HERITAGE UNLOCKED

Guide to free sites in London
and the South East

St Catherine's Oratory, Isle of Wight

CONTENTS

INTRODUCTION

As well as major attractions, which include Apsley House in London and Dover Castle in Kent, English Heritage has many sites in London and the South East of England where entry is free. This book, one of a series of regional guidebooks, provides a useful introduction to each of these free sites.

Among the region's oldest monuments are the burial chambers and mounds built by its earliest farming communities, such as those at Wayland's Smithy and Kit's Coty. The origins and functions of many of these ancient sites – which also include the huge, leaping White Horse cut into the hillside in Oxfordshire – remain mysterious.

The Romans first stepped on to British shores near Richborough and Reculver, Kent, where they built forts. St Augustine's Cross in Kent marks the arrival of St Augustine in the 6th century and the resurgence of the Christian faith, seen in the building of churches and monasteries.

Following the Norman Conquest castles for defence also became part of the landscape. Manor houses such as Minster Lovell in Oxfordshire testify to the wealth and power of the leading families of the region in the Middle Ages.

Many families benefited from the Dissolution of the Monasteries, gaining monastic lands and buildings for their own private use: in Hampshire, Netley Abbey was converted into a house, while Waverley Abbey in Surrey was ransacked for stone and reduced to ruin.

A range of later architectural styles is represented in the baroque Abingdon County Hall, Oxfordshire, and the neoclassical mansion Northington Grange, Hampshire. Throughout the book, special features highlight additional aspects of the region's history and character, such as its industrial and literary heritage, and the statues that enliven the streets of London.

This guide aims to help visitors to explore and enjoy some of the lesser-known but intriguing monuments in English Heritage's care. A brief guide to English Heritage's admission-charging sites in London and the South East is also given.

View of the stairwell at Dungeness Lighthouse, Kent

LONDON

London, the largest city in the British Isles, capital of a nation and formerly of an empire, was first inhabited some 350,000 years ago. The city developed here over 2,000 years ago largely because of the convenience of crossing points over the River Thames, the main artery of commerce. Though London lost significance as a river port in the 20th century, mercantile traditions have continued to dominate activity within the Square Mile, still the base for many international corporations and banks, and in shopping districts around the West End. Incorporating the once separate City of Westminster, London has been a place of government since the Roman occupation. It remains the setting for many national rituals of state and religion, with its palaces of the powerful and rich, imposing public buildings and monuments commemorating the events and personalities responsible for shaping the nation's history. As home to a large

and varied population and attracting visitors from all over the world, London has a vibrant tradition of cultural diversity. This tradition is reflected in the differing characters of its residential districts and in its eclectic architecture. Although the pace of development may seem to have accelerated to an unprecedented speed, the same challenge which faces London at the turn of the 21st century can be detected at many stages in its history: the need to reinvent itself as a modern city, but at the same time to retain those elements of history and tradition which have made it a great city of unique character.

Right: View over the River Thames, looking east

Central London contains more than 500 public statues and monuments. Some are famous landmarks, such as the Cenotaph, Nelson's Column or Piccadilly Circus's *Eros*, but many are now little noticed, merging into the streetscape. Yet all were charged with meaning for those who commissioned and made them.

The practice of erecting public statues derives from Classical Greece and Rome but it can come as a surprise to realise how recent most of London's statues are: the majority of them date from after 1870.

Medieval England had a rich tradition of both religious and secular sculpture, though little of this survives to the present day. Regardless of subject matter, medieval sculpture was destroyed on a massive scale by Protestant iconoclasts in the 16th and 17th centuries. The figures of kings that survive in the interior of Westminster Hall, and the Guildhall porch sculpture, now in the Museum of London, are among the very few remaining examples.

The first public statue in London was probably the figure of Charles I in Trafalgar Square by the French sculptor Hubert le Sueur. Commissioned to adorn a private garden, it was made in 1633 but only put up as a public monument in 1676. Over the following 150 years a handful of statues were erected in London: figures of monarchs wearing Roman armour and philanthropists standing outside the hospitals and almshouses which they supported. The preferred form of commemorating eminent individuals in the 18th century was by white marble tomb monuments. The most spectacular collection

Left: King Charles I, Trafalgar Square

Right: Emmeline Pankhurst, Victoria Tower Gardens

of such sculpture survives in Westminster Abbey, which gradually turned into a form of national mausoleum.

The idea of commemorating individuals with public monuments received its greatest impetus in the 19th century after Britain's victory over Napoleonic France, which inspired several memorials to Horatio, Viscount Nelson, and Arthur Wellesley, first Duke of Wellington. Victorian patriotism and imperial expansion led to other military heroes being similarly honoured, but it was not long before figures celebrating people regarded as embodying other Victorian values – of liberal individualism, material

progress and service to civilisation – began to make their mark. By the 1860s statues of poets, statesmen, doctors, engineers and explorers, among others, were also appearing in the city. The period from 1875 to 1914 was the high point of this culture of commemoration. Perhaps the best-known public monument of the Victorian age is the Albert Memorial, commemorating the Prince Consort, in Hyde Park. Designed by George Gilbert Scott, it was completed in 1872 and unveiled in 1876. The memorial was reopened in 1998 after an extensive four-year conservation programme by English Heritage.

Uncertainty about the nature and value of fame can be seen in many late 20th-century memorials, and future directions for memorial sculpture remain unclear. What is clear, however, is that London's public statues form a valuable artistic and historical legacy.

Above left: The Albert Memorial, Hyde Park

Right: Bust of Nelson Mandela, Royal Festival Hall, South Bank

7

Coombe Conduit represents an intriguing survival from the system which, for 350 years, provided fresh water to Hampton Court Palace.

History

The Hampton Court conduit system was fed from three conduit heads, which were known as Coombe Conduit, Gallows Conduit and Ivy Conduit (the last is not in English Heritage's guardianship). The system

has traditionally been attributed to Cardinal Thomas Wolsey, who began work to the great palace at Hampton Court between 1514 and 1529. More recent research has suggested that the system was installed during Henry VIII's residence, from 1529 onwards. This is further supported by the fact that the lands on which the conduit heads were built belonged until 1538 to Merton Priory: after the suppression of the monastery, these lands fell into the king's hands.

The Coombe Conduit system supplied the palace with water until 1876, though the supply had become intermittent some time before. In 1896 the conduit houses and a length of the lead piping were sold to the Duke of Cambridge, on whose land they stood. In 1900 the Crown formally relinquished all rights over the pipes.

The upper conduit house at Coombe Conduit was badly damaged in 1943 when an elm tree, weakened by high-explosive bombs, fell across the west and north walls, bringing down the remains of the roof, the two masonry gables and parts of the remainder of the walls. This damage was partly repaired under the War Damage Act and fully restored in 1956, after a lengthy debate about conservation philosophy.

In about 1970 the area was developed residentially, and Coombe

Conduit was enclosed within the garden of 28 Lord Chancellor's Way.

Description

Coombe Conduit originally consisted of an upper and a lower chamber, 20m (65.5ft) apart, connected by an underground vaulted passage. Water from the spring passed into a tank in the upper chamber, from which it was drawn by a pipe into a tank in the lower chamber. Here sediment was allowed to settle. From the lower tank the water passed into the main conduit leading to the palace. Intermediate tanks fitted with stopcocks enabled sections of pipe to be isolated for repairs. The total length of piping was about 5.5km (18,000 ft). The lead pipes were of three-inch diameter and half an inch (1.25cm) thick. The system was engineered with a fall of 39.3m (129ft) over a length of about 4.8km (3 miles), creating a water pressure adequate to supply running water to rooms on the second floor of the palace.

In the 17th century an additional tank was created on the north side of the upper chamber at a lower level than the Tudor original, with a third tank being added in the 18th century on the south side.

***Above**: The passage leading to the middle chamber*

E of Kingston upon Thames on A238; junction of Coombe Lane West with Lord Chancellor's Way
OS Map 176, ref TQ 204698
Open Apr–Sep, every second Sun: 2–4pm

Above: Portrait of William Murray, Earl of Mansfield, *by Jan Baptiste van Loo, about 1742*

Right: *Robert Adam's library at Kenwood*

Facing page: *The south front of Kenwood from the south-west*

Between 1764 and 1779 the architect Robert Adam remodelled and extended an existing house to create a villa in the neoclassical style for the greatest British judge of the 18th century, William Murray, first Earl of Mansfield. Located on the edge of Hampstead Heath, with fine views over London, Kenwood stands today in 45 hectares (112 acres) of gardens and ancient woodland, providing a unique setting in which to enjoy some of the world's greatest art.

Kenwood was not the country seat of a landed dynasty but rather the suburban home of a self-made and highly successful lawyer. This is reflected in the relative modesty of the entrance hall when compared with those by Adam in houses designed for the nobility, such as Syon Park in Brentford or Kedleston Hall in Derbyshire. The decoration of the room alludes to Bacchus, the Roman god of wine – this room also doubled as a dining room, tables being set up for the occasion and removed after each meal.

On stepping from the entrance hall through the stairwell into the antechamber the visitor enters the extension to the older house that was added by Adam between 1767 and 1770. This culminates in the dramatic

library, or Great Room, designed to serve both as a library and as a room for receiving company. It is Adam's masterpiece and one of the finest 18th-century British interiors.

Two further wings were added to the house between 1793 and 1796 by Murray's nephew and successor, the second Earl of Mansfield, to provide the dining room and drawing room, or music room, with bedrooms above. It is in these wings that the finest paintings from the collection of Lord Iveagh are displayed. These include masterpieces by Rembrandt, Vermeer, Hals, Van Dyck, Gainsborough, Reynolds and Turner. This collection was formed at the end of the 19th century by Edward Cecil Guinness, first Earl of Iveagh, chairman of the Guinness brewery, who bought Kenwood in 1925. He died shortly afterwards, bequeathing the house and the collection to the nation.

Along the south front of Kenwood, bordering the terrace, is a suite of rooms comprising the former family apartments. At the western end is the

orangery, which was formerly a free-standing greenhouse. Adam linked this building to the main house by means of an antechamber. Adam designed the library as a symmetrical counterpart to the orangery, so giving the villa an elegant long facade that commands a panoramic prospect of the London skyline.

The pastoral 18th-century landscape around the house was transformed in the 1790s by the landscape architect Humphry Repton, at the request of the second earl. At this time the former service buildings to the north-east of the house were replaced by a new service wing, stables, gate lodges and dairy, all of which survive today.

Hampstead Lane, NW3
OS Map 176, ref TQ 271874
Open
31 Mar–31 Oct:
11am–5pm
daily;
1 Nov–31 Mar:
11am–4pm
daily; closed
24–26 Dec
and 1 Jan
Tel: 020 8348 1286

Immediately to the north of the Tower of London stands one of the most substantial and impressive surviving sections of the Roman wall around the city of London.

From its earliest foundation the Roman city of Londinium was almost certainly surrounded by some kind of fortification. As well as providing defence, the construction of a stone wall represented the status of the city.

Using the evidence of excavated coins, archaeologists have dated the construction of the first stone city wall to between AD 190 and 225. The wall was about 4km (2.5 miles) long, enclosing an area of about 134 hectares (330 acres); it originally included four city gates with an additional entrance into the legionary fortress at Cripplegate. In front of the eastern face of the wall was a ditch, which was up to 1.8m (6ft) deep and 4.8m (16ft) across.

This section of the wall stood close to the south-east corner of the ditch, now lying inside the bailey of the Tower of London. It is built of rubble (mostly Kentish ragstone) bound in a hard mortar, and faced on either side by roughly squared ragstone blocks. At every fifth or sixth

The Roman wall with the Tower of London beyond

course the wall incorporates a horizontal band of red Roman tiles, intended to ensure the courses remained level over long stretches of masonry. This gives the wall its distinctive striped appearance.

This section shows signs of medieval alteration, particularly in its upper portions, and its original height is unknown; but at about 10.7m (35ft) above present ground level it is one of the tallest surviving sections parts of the circuit.

The wall was originally built without the external D-shaped bastions or turrets which can be seen in several places around the city: these were added in the 4th century, almost certainly as emplacements for catapults or stone-throwing engines. One of these bastions, immediately to the north of the standing section of wall, has been found to incorporate reused stonework. This includes parts of a monument bearing the inscription of Julius Alpinus Classicianus, procurator of Britain, who was responsible for the

reconstruction of London after the chaos of Boudicca's rebellion of AD 60 and its violent aftermath. The dismantling of this monument indicates the urgency with which the wall was strengthened in the later

Reconstruction drawing of the defensive circuit around London in about AD 370

View along the section of the wall from the south

Roman period. The reconstructed Classicianus monument is now displayed in the British Museum, although a replica can be viewed on the site.

The Roman wall remained standing after the departure of the Roman army in 410, through a long period during which the city seems to have been largely abandoned. It was repaired in the late Anglo-Saxon period and survived to be an important feature of the city plan at the time of the Norman Conquest of 1066. Large parts of the wall were incorporated into the medieval defences of the city. In about 1300 a new postern gateway through the wall was built immediately to the south of the standing portion, close to the edge of the Tower of London moat; it later slipped down the moat bank and can be seen at the end of the underpass under the main road.

The Roman wall continued to influence the development of the city street plan through the Middle Ages and beyond. By the mid-17th century

buildings had been erected against sections of the wall on either side. In time it was obscured and, later, partly destroyed during the construction of new buildings and railway lines.

In 1938 the wall and part of the land on its western side were placed in the guardianship of the Ministry of Works. Since the 1930s several buildings which had formerly hidden this section of the wall have been cleared away, revealing it to view.

Close to the Thames and surrounded by Victorian warehouses and modern office blocks stand the fragmentary remains of a great medieval palace, the London residence of the rich and powerful Bishops of Winchester.

History

Winchester Palace was founded in the 12th century by Bishop Henry of Blois, brother of King Stephen. One of the richest and most powerful churchmen in England, he was the builder of other spectacular palaces, including Wolvesey (see pp. 84–7), close to his cathedral in Winchester. Winchester Palace was intended to house the bishop and his household in fitting style and comfort, within easy reach of the royal court in Westminster. It was much extended in the early 13th century by Peter des Roches, Chancellor of England and tutor to Henry III. A contemporary said of Bishop Peter that he was 'more interested in lucre than Saint Luke, and in the value of a mark than Saint Mark'; here, characteristically,

the bishop provided himself and his household with substantial accommodation, arranged around two courtyards.

Later in the Middle Ages and under the Tudors the palace fell into disrepair and the riverside area in this part of London gained a reputation for lawlessness and immorality. The

The west gable wall of the great hall of Winchester Palace on Clink Street

most notorious feature of the palace, the bishop's prison, was immortalised under the name 'The Clink', commemorated in the name of the street along the palace's northern side. By the 17th century the Bishops of Winchester used the palace infrequently. In the Civil War it was seized by the new Parliament for use as a prison, later to be sold into private hands. Although it was restored to the bishops after the Commonwealth, no real attempt was made to revive it as a palace. In the 18th century the various tenements within the palace changed hands many times, though the site remained the property of the diocese of Winchester. In the late 18th and early 19th centuries the area of the great hall and kitchen was let to Messrs Lingard and Sadler, manufacturers of mustard.

On 28 August 1814, Lingard and Sadler's premises were gutted by fire. As a result the remains of the medieval buildings were revealed, and several artists and antiquarians took the opportunity to make recording drawings. The ruins themselves were almost immediately hidden again by new brick warehouses. In 1941 the warehouse to the west of the medieval hall was damaged by a parachute mine and afterwards demolished. The period after the war saw the gradual removal of other buildings and several

The hall range of Winchester Palace in its setting by the river, from Wenceslas Hollar's Panorama of London, 1647

archaeological excavations have provided invaluable information about the form and development of the palace. In the late 1960s the surviving remains of the west end of the great hall passed into the guardianship of the Ministry of Works.

Description

The standing remains, mostly dating to the early 13th century and the period of Peter des Roches, were built as part of a long range running east–west along what was then the south bank of the Thames. This range, which was 87m (285ft) long, incorporated several buildings, including kitchens and a great hall, set over a cellar into which goods could be carried directly from a wharf on the river. Behind the riverside range stood two courtyards containing service buildings and accommodation for the household, and a large garden for the bishop's use.

The largest surviving fragment of the fabric of Winchester Palace is the west gable wall, which divided the great hall from the kitchens and service rooms. It contains three doors at what was then the main floor level, leading to the buttery, pantry and kitchen. Part of the south wall of the hall also survives, containing doors into the hall and cellar; parts of the mouldings of the upper hall show an architectural similarity to contemporary buildings, such as the great hall of Winchester Castle, which Bishop Peter built for Henry III in the 1230s.

The most distinctive feature surviving in the great hall is the circular window set high in the gable. It dates from the late 13th or early 14th century, when the upper parts of the wall were evidently taken down and rebuilt. The window's design, with radiating spokes in the centre and intersecting triangles with elaborate ornamental cusping, is unique in England and Wales.

The rose window high in the west gable wall at Winchester Palace

Next to Southwark Cathedral and the Golden Hinde replica ship; corner of Clink Street and Storey Street, SE1

OS Map 177, ref TQ 325803

'Sweet Thames! run softly, till I end
my song …'

The Thames has always dominated London life. This famous line is from the poet Edmund Spenser's celebration of the river in his *Prothalamion*, published in 1596. T S Eliot, in *The Waste Land* (1922), reused Spenser's words, and evoked the city and its river at different moments in history. Eliot mused on the crowd that 'flowed over London Bridge' while the poet William Wordsworth, writing over a century earlier in 1802, had described a deserted scene 'so touching in its majesty' in *Westminster Bridge*.

For the last six years of his life J M W Turner, who had been appointed the Royal Academy's Professor of Perspective in 1807, lived and painted incognito as 'Mr Booth' in Cheyne Walk in Chelsea, drawn there, like James McNeill Whistler after him, by the river views and clear light. In Leicester Square the painter and engraver William Hogarth had his studio, and it was here that he completed his satirical series *The Rake's Progress* (1734), now in Sir John Soane's Museum. The series tells the story of the fictional Tom Rakewell who pursues pleasure and advancement in London but ends his life in Bedlam Hospital. The painter and poet William Blake spent his early life in Soho, the 'charter'd streets' of which feature in his 1794 poem *London*. England's best-known artistic movement was born in Bloomsbury in 1848. Here, in Gower Street, Dante Gabriel Rossetti, Sir John Everett Millais and William Holman Hunt founded the Pre-Raphaelite Brotherhood, dedicated to a 'crusade and holy warfare against the present age'.

Charles Dickens was also a Bloomsbury

Left: Painting by Edward Matthew Ward (1816–79) of Hogarth's Studio in 1739

resident for much of his life. In his childhood he lived in Gower Street and shortly after his marriage moved to a house in Doughty Street, where he began to establish his literary reputation. The house is now a museum to him. In Tavistock Square, where Dickens had lived later in life, Virginia and Leonard Woolf founded the Hogarth Press and lived at the centre of the Bloomsbury Group, an intellectual circle including E M Forster and Lytton Strachey. Virginia Woolf's novel *Mrs Dalloway* (1923) is a powerful evocation of London after the First World War.

George Orwell was also in London in the 1920s, sometimes choosing to sleep rough and working at various poorly paid jobs, as he described in *Down and Out in Paris and London* (1933). In his novel *1984* (1948) he based the 'Ministry of Truth' on London University's Senate House and the 'Ministry of Love' on the former Bethnal Green Police Station. The poet John Betjeman celebrated his 1920s Highgate childhood in *Summoned by Bells*. Different Londons have been sketched by more recent writers. In *The Lonely Londoners* (1956) the novelist Sam Selvon followed the experience of black immigrants in Earls Court and Bayswater. More recently, Monica Ali has charted the life of an east London community in *Brick Lane* (2003). Peter Ackroyd's ambitious *London: The Biography* (2000) is the city's life story, but the 18th-century writer Samuel Johnson demands to have the last word: 'When a man is tired of London he is tired of life; for there is in London all that life can afford.'

Above: Virginia Woolf in a portrait by her sister, Vanessa Bell, 1912
Below: *An etching of Westminster Bridge, before 1834 (artist unknown)*

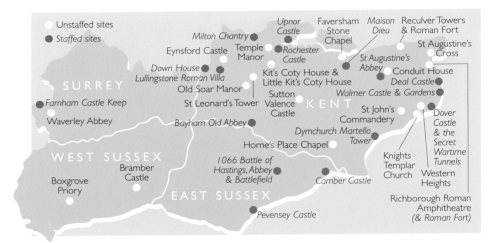

○ Unstaffed sites
● Staffed sites

Milton Chantry
Eynsford Castle
Temple Manor
Upnor Castle
Faversham Stone Chapel
Maison Dieu
Reculver Towers & Roman Fort
St Augustine's Cross
Rochester Castle
Down House
Lullingstone Roman Villa
St Augustine's Abbey
Conduit House
Old Soar Manor
Kit's Coty House & Little Kit's Coty House
Deal Castle
Farnham Castle Keep
St Leonard's Tower
Sutton Valence Castle
Walmer Castle & Gardens
Waverley Abbey
SURREY
KENT
St John's Commandery
Bayham Old Abbey
Dover Castle & the Secret Wartime Tunnels
Dymchurch Martello Tower
Home's Place Chapel
Knights Templar Church
Western Heights
WEST SUSSEX
Bramber Castle
1066 Battle of Hastings, Abbey & Battlefield
Boxgrove Priory
Camber Castle
EAST SUSSEX
Richborough Roman Amphitheatre (& Roman Fort)
Pevensey Castle

Since the formation of the English Channel about 8,000 years ago, the counties of the South East have been both the site of invasion by forces from the Continent and also a first point of contact between England and the rest of Europe. In prehistory trade with the Continent was conducted from the shores of Kent and Sussex. In AD 43 the Romans' main entry point into Britain was at Richborough in Kent, and the extent of the remains there bear witness to its importance throughout the period of Roman occupation. At nearby Pegwell Bay, Christianity was reintroduced to England in 597 by St Augustine, and Canterbury remains at the centre of the Anglican faith.

Perhaps the most significant event in the history of England occurred with the

Farm buildings and oast houses at Whitbread Hop Farm, Paddock Wood, Kent

invasion in 1066 by William, Duke of Normandy, at Pevensey and his subsequent defeat of King Harold at the battle of Hastings. Castles large and small were built by the Normans to control the native population.

In later centuries, continued tensions between Britain and Europe led to the building of extensive fortifications, such as the Martello towers intended to repel potential attacks by Napoleonic forces. In 1940 the South East earned a special place in the nation's history as the frontline in the Battle of Britain. More recent monuments are, however, once again those of trade and international relations: the Channel Tunnel, the port of Dover, and Gatwick Airport.

CONDUIT HOUSE

The remains of this medieval conduit house stand in King's Park, Canterbury, on a steep west-facing hillside to the east of St Augustine's Abbey (see p. 123), whose spring water supply it was built to protect.

A reliable supply of fresh water was an essential element of the infrastructure of a monastic community. The location of rivers and streams was often a significant factor in deciding the precise site of monastic houses, but within a town local supplies might be polluted. In such cases clean water had to be piped in from a spring; the water flowed through pipes that were made of lead or hollowed-out tree trunks. Arrangements such as this were well known in the medieval period. Sources of water on a higher level than the monastery were tapped and small buildings were constructed to cover the collecting and settling tanks at the spring.

The conduit house at St Augustine's Abbey dates from the mid-12th century. A roughly octagonal masonry tank is now divided by an 18th-century chalk and brick wall. Four tunnelled openings and three smaller ducts, which collect water from springs, lead into the tank. Water was delivered from here to the abbey by a lead pipe 75cm (3in.) in diameter running from the western side of the structure. The pipe may have led to a water tower at the abbey, which would have fed smaller tanks in the kitchen, infirmary and other parts of the monastic complex. The walls of the tank, which survive to a height of

The remains of the mid-12th-century conduit house – water was collected in the masonry tank

approximately 3m (10ft), are built of flint and chalk blocks on chalk block foundations. The internal wall faces are of coursed flint and were originally rendered. The bed of the tank is of natural earth, with a high clay content.

In the 18th century, when the holding tank was divided, a new roof was constructed, consisting of two shallow barrel vaults. This may have been the work of Sir John Hales, who, in 1773, allowed Canterbury the use of the reservoir which he then owned to supplement its water supply.

In February 1988 the roof of the conduit house collapsed, though the tank and access tunnels can still be seen.

St Augustine's Abbey is a five- to ten-minute walk away to the west.

The ruins of St Augustine's Abbey, from the south-east. The conduit house supplied the abbey with fresh water

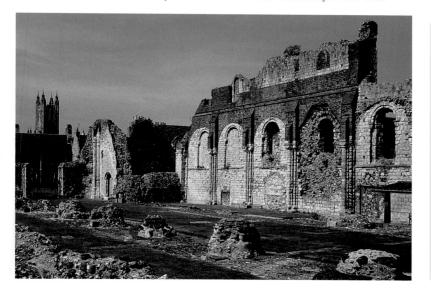

In Canterbury: from ring road turn right into Havelock Street, right into North Holmes Road, left into St Martin's Road, right into King's Park. External viewing only
OS Map 179, ref TR 159580

Facing page: The
remains of the
medieval hall house
at Eynsford Castle

The ruins of Eynsford Castle stand
on the east bank of the River Darent,
in a valley which cuts through an area
of gently undulating chalk downland.
The castle is situated in the village
of Eynsford, and the peace of its
surroundings today obscures the
sometimes turbulent medieval history
of the site.

History

Eynsford is an example of an early
form of Norman castle known as an
enclosure castle. This was a type of
building defended principally by a
strong wall surrounding the site.

The earliest defensive structure
on the site, possibly predating the
Norman Conquest of 1066, was
composed of a timber watchtower
on an artificial motte, or mound. No
evidence of this can be seen today.
The curtain wall was constructed in
about 1090 by William de Eynsford.
In 1130 the wall was heightened
and a gate-tower was built to
strengthen the defences. A hall,
which provided accommodation for
the Eynsford family, was also
constructed. After a fire in about
1250 this was reconstructed and new
kitchens were built.

The line of the Eynsford family which owned the castle died out in the 13th century and the castle became the subject of a disputed inheritance. In 1312 it was attacked by one of the claimants and documentary evidence records a complaint about the doors and windows of the castle having been broken down, damage caused and cattle let loose. Court actions followed but no compromise was reached, and the castle was never inhabited again. For some time it was used as a manorial court but the buildings gradually fell into disrepair. It was last used in the 18th century, as stables and kennels for hunting dogs.

Description

A low oval platform is enclosed by the curtain wall with a moat to the north, east and south. To the west the castle was protected by the river. The wall, constructed mainly of flint, stands to a height of 9m (29ft) and is almost 2m (7ft) wide at its base. The north-west segment has collapsed and remains where it fell.

Within the wall are the remains of the hall, built in the 12th century. This was a comfortable dwelling house with domestic quarters above an undercroft, or vaulted cellar. Excavation has revealed that the hall had glazed windows, an early instance of glass being used in a domestic building and indicative of the wealth and high status of the owners. Like the curtain wall, the building was constructed mostly of flint, with some reused Roman tiles brought from the remains of Roman villas nearby.

The remains of a well and separate kitchen building in the castle can also be seen. The foundations of the gatehouse mark the site of a bridge over the moat.

In Eynsford
off A225
OS Map 177,
ref TQ 542658
Open
31 Mar–30 Sep:
10am–6pm;
1 Oct–30 Nov:
10am–4pm;
1 Dec–31 Jan:
10am–4pm,
Wed–Sun;
1 Feb–31 Mar:
10am–4pm

At Stone-by-Faversham a medieval chapel was built on top of a Roman mausoleum – a very rare occurrence. The chapel stands isolated in a shallow, dry valley within open fields. The Roman Watling Street, now the busy A2, runs adjacent to the field 100m (330ft) south of the site. It is thought that the Roman settlement of Durolevum was situated on the outskirts of Faversham, and the only upstanding remains possibly relating to this settlement exist in this ruined chapel. The chapel fell into disuse in the 16th century. The nave and eastern part of the chancel are medieval but the western half of the chancel is Roman.

The Roman mausoleum

The Roman building was excavated during the 19th century and again in the 1960s and 1970s. It was found to be a roughly square structure with each side approximately 6m (17ft) in length, built on a foundation raft of flints. The walls are 1m (3ft) thick and are constructed of square stone blocks with frequent courses of thin red bricks. The walls were reinforced with external buttresses, two of which survive, at the north-west and south-west corners of the building. The original entrance is represented by a gap in the centre of the west wall, with the original sill – a slab of greensand stone – still in place. Internally the floor was constructed of *opus signinum* (a hard waterproof concrete partly composed of, and coloured red with, crushed tiles) and the walls were decorated with red painted plaster.

The east end of the medieval chapel, which made use of the surviving Roman walls

This building has been interpreted as a Romano-British mausoleum, a tomb standing above ground. Mausolea were constructed to contain and mark high-status burials. They often served as family tombs, in which some form of ceremony could be performed when a new burial was placed in the monument. They are usually located within cemeteries but may also be found singly, associated with villas or in small groups. The tradition of building mausolea in Britain began in the early 2nd century AD and continued until at least the 4th century.

As there is no evidence of a villa or cemetery close by, it has also been suggested that the building was a Romano-British temple or small Christian shrine. Excavations have revealed a further Roman building about 11m (36ft) to the north-west.

The medieval church

Partially overlying the earlier Roman building, but making use of its surviving walls, are the ruins of a mainly flint-built medieval church, about 24m (78ft) in length and up to 7.5m (25ft) wide. There may have been an earlier timber-built Saxon church on the site. The medieval builders used the Roman building as the chancel of the church, while the nave was built to the west. The nave and the chancel were extended in the 13th century. The church is surrounded by a roughly square graveyard, bounded by a flint wall, which survives in ruined form on the north-western side and elsewhere is marked in places by a low bank. The church was abandoned by the 1530s.

View of the chapel from the south

1¼ miles W of Faversham on A2
OS Map 178, ref TQ 992613

27

Horne's Place Chapel is situated on low-lying ground north of the village of Appledore on the western edge of Romney Marsh. It forms the earliest standing wing of the attached manor house, which is a private dwelling.

History

Horne's Place was the seat of the influential Horne family from 1276, when Edward I granted land containing the manor to Matthew Horne. The chapel was licensed for divine service in 1366. A domestic chapel allowed a family to attend services conveniently at home rather than obliging them to travel to the parish church, and receipt of the licence for worship was an indicator of the family's high status.

During Wat Tyler's rising in 1381 the manor house was forcibly entered and valuable goods were stolen. William Horne, then owner of the house and a Justice of the Peace, was

Horne's Place Chapel viewed from the south-east

made one of the commissioners responsible for crushing the revolt in Kent. Later, the chapel fell out of religious use. It was used as a barn in the 19th and early 20th centuries.

Description

The small, high building, measuring approximately 8m by 4m (26ft by 13ft) and constructed of Kentish ragstone, is arranged on two floors.

The chapel rests on a partly sunken undercroft, or vaulted cellar, used originally for storage. The undercroft is entered by way of modern steps through a pointed-arched doorway. It has a stone-flagged floor (below which two burials were discovered) and access to a well. The chapel was linked to the hall wing of the manor house by a doorway, now blocked, in its north wall.

Significant alterations took place in the early 16th century. The brick barrel vault of the undercroft dates to this period, when a gallery was also constructed at the west end of the chapel. This has been removed but the joist holes on the west wall indicate its position.

The gallery was linked to the ground floor by an external spiral staircase, which has also been removed. The blocked door which led to the gallery can be seen above the present entrance to the chapel, which is also a 16th-century modification as indicated by the yellow bricks forming the doorway.

The three main lights of the chapel's large restored east window are decorated with cinquefoil cusping. The architectural historian Nikolaus Pevsner describes the details of this 'exquisite little building' as being 'of the utmost refinement, far above the level of the local parish churches'.

The present roof of the chapel dates from the 1520s. The main roof trusses are supported on stone corbels decorated with Catherine wheels. This motif suggests that the chapel may have been dedicated to St Catherine.

The chapel adjoins a private house and garden. The owners ask visitors to respect their privacy by making prior arrangements to visit. Please telephone the English Heritage reception at Dover Castle, Kent, on 01304 211067.

The restored east window of the chapel

1½ miles N of Appledore
OS Map 189, ref TQ 958309

Industry in the South East has long been dominated by the needs of the nation's capital. The strategic demands of London led to the development of naval dockyards, first at Deptford and then around the coast at Chatham, Sheerness and Portsmouth, which all retain reminders of their former glory. Less obvious are the remains of the client industries, such as explosives and gun-founding. The gunpowder mills around Faversham and in the Chilworth valley can still be visited but the historic iron industry of the Weald has left only

slight remains, such as the hammer ponds – which supplied water for mill-driven forge hammers – and cast-iron tombstones at Wadhurst.

The former importance of coastal trade is witnessed by lighthouses such as the one at Beachy Head, by the wharves and warehouses of Faversham and Rye, by the net shops of Hastings and by the harbours of Margate, Dover and Portsmouth. The pleasure piers at Gravesend, Herne Bay, Eastbourne, Brighton, Bognor and Shanklin were originally built as landing stages. The Thames, as the focus of inland navigation, has fine bridges, locks and weirs, while the River Kennet's turf-sided locks on the Kennet and Avon link to Bristol and the River Wey's treadwheel crane at Guildford are unique survivors of the industrial past.

Above: *The Chart Gunpowder Mills, Faversham, Kent*

Left: *Samuel Bentham's revolutionary Block Mills at Portsmouth Royal Naval Dockyard*

Radiating out of London, the railways have made their mark on the landscape: examples include Robert Stephenson's pioneering engineering works and settlement at Wolverton for the London and Birmingham Railway, Brunel's graceful bridges at Maidenhead, Moulsford and Basildon for the Great Western Railway and his Windsor branch, with the iron bowstring-girder bridge and Royal Waiting Room. On the route to the south coast the Ouse Viaduct and Clayton Tunnel are prominent features, while the 19th-century Ashford Railway Works sits incongruously alongside the modern Eurostar station.

The remains of agricultural industries catering for both London and the regions abound. Among the many windmills are those at Brill, Lacey Green and Pitstone in Buckinghamshire, at Chillenden, Cranbrook and Rolvenden in Kent, at Outwood in Surrey, at Nutley, Polegate and Clayton in Sussex, at Bursledon in Hampshire and at Bembridge on the Isle of Wight. As important, if less prominent as a feature in the landscape, are watermills, such as those at Farnham, Guildford, Shalford, Hellingley, Robertsbridge, Eling and Winchester. Oast houses for drying hops, such as those at Chestfield, Pembury and Sissinghurst, are iconic features of the Kent and north-east Hampshire landscapes.

Above left: Brunel's railway bridge at Maidenhead

Below: Oasthouses near Chilham, Kent, in 1956

Kit's Coty House and Little Kit's Coty House are the remains of two megalithic long barrows standing in open fields. The sites offer fine long views across the North Downs and Medway Valley.

The origin of the name Kit's Coty is not known. For many years it was thought to be a corruption of Catigern, the name of a British prince slain in single combat with the Saxon Horsa in a battle at Aylesford in 455 at which the Britons were victorious.

The burial chamber at Kit's Coty House

The monuments were therefore assumed to be a memorial to him. There is no evidence to support this suggestion and the barrows predate this event by thousands of years.

Long barrows were constructed during the early Neolithic period, between about 4000 and 3000 BC. They represent the burial places of the earliest farming communities in Britain, and are among the oldest surviving prehistoric monuments. Long barrows appear to have been used for communal burial – often with only parts of the human remains being selected for interment – and it is probable that they acted as important ritual sites for local communities over a considerable period of time.

Kit's Coty House

The most distinctive surviving feature of this monument is the H-shaped arrangement of three large slabs of sarsen stone (a fine-grained, crystalline sandstone) capped by a further slab, which formed the main

Little Kit's Coty House viewed from the south-east

W of A229
2 miles N of
Maidstone.
Approach from N,
where North
Downs Way meets
northbound slip
road to A229. Kit's
Coty House lies
to W of footpath,
200m down hill.
Little Kit's Coty
House lies 450m
further down hill,
on S side of road
to Aylesford.
*OS Map 188,
refs TQ 745608
and TQ 744604*

burial chamber of the barrow. The stones would originally have been buried at the eastern end of a long earthen mound, of which only traces survive. Earth and chalk for the construction of this mound was quarried from flanking ditches to the north and south and these can be seen clearly on aerial photographs of the site. The mound was surrounded by a retaining kerb of sarsens, some of which may be buried in the field.

Little Kit's Coty House

Little Kit's Coty House, also known as the Countless Stones, is a group of about 20 sarsen stones in a tight cluster. They represent the remains of a burial mound which was seriously damaged in 1690, before any reliable records were made. A letter written at the time describes '13 or 14 great stones, 7 standing all covered with one large stone'. It is likely that this burial chamber was originally covered with a substantial mound, as at Kit's Coty House. In the 1880s, as concern mounted about damage to ancient monuments, Kit's Coty House and Little Kit's Coty House were among the first to be protected by the state, on the advice of General Augustus Henry Lane Fox Pitt-Rivers, the first Inspector of Ancient Monuments. Railings were erected around the stones to prevent vandalism.

33

Right: An artist's impression of a Knight Templar in the uniform of the order, as depicted in an engraving of the 17th or 18th century

Below: Knights Templar Church from the west

On the
Western Heights
above Dover
OS Map 179,
ref TR 313407

Standing on the Western Heights above Dover are the stone foundations of a small chapel, which has been linked to the Knights Templar.

The Knights Templar were a military and religious order founded in the 12th century, during the Crusades, to protect pilgrims travelling to the Holy Land and to defend the holy places there. They became rich and powerful but increasingly unpopular, and the order was eventually suppressed in 1312. The port of Dover, the chief departure point for pilgrimages to the Holy Land, would have been an obvious place for the Templars to have held property, but they are believed to have left the town before 1185 and their links to this particular site are tenuous. An alternative interpretation suggests that the building was a wayside shrine on the Dover to Folkestone road.

The chapel, built in the 12th century, had a circular nave 10m (33ft) in diameter and a rectangular chancel. The form mirrors that of the Church of the Holy Sepulchre in Jerusalem, and it is this association that has suggested the link with the Templars. Their most complete church, though much restored, is the Temple Church in London.

The buried foundations were discovered in the early 19th century during the construction of the Western Heights military defences (see pp. 54–5). Only the flint and mortar core of the foundations and a small area of stone facing survive.

Old Soar Manor is situated in a remote position in the Kent countryside near Ightham, on the edge of the North Downs.

History

This rare survival of 13th-century domestic architecture gives an illuminating impression of the life of a rich medieval family. The manor belonged to the Culpeppers, a leading Kentish family in the Middle Ages who were major landowners.

Manor houses of this period were based around a great hall, with a central fire from which the smoke rose to the open rafters. Family and servants would have eaten in the hall and servants slept on the floor. The manorial court would also have been

Left: Old Soar Manor from the east

held here. For privacy, the lord and his close family would retire to withdrawing rooms, often a parlour with a solar, or upper chamber, above.

Today the private quarters of the Culpeppers survive, although the timber hall to which these rooms were attached was demolished in 1780 and the surviving red-brick farmhouse built in its place (the farmhouse is privately owned and is not open to the public).

Description

The building was constructed in about 1290 of roughly coursed Kentish ragstone. It consists of a solar, latrine and small private chapel. All three rooms stand above vaulted undercrofts, or cellars, which were used for storage.

The solar was reached by a spiral staircase leading out of the hall. It has a steeply pitched crown-post roof. Each end wall features a long window. These would not originally have been glazed, but closed by shutters, the fittings for which can still be seen.

A window seat survives below the northern window. This room, in contrast to the hall, had a square chimneybreast and fireplace. A blocked doorway or window opposite the fireplace overlooked the hall. A smaller blocked window would have allowed the lord discreetly to observe activity in the hall below. A latrine, leading off the solar, discharged into a pit on the outside of the building. This room may also have been used to store clothes, as the odour of urine was believed to keep away pests.

The chapel has a large window which, in contrast to those in the rest of the house, was completely glazed. It once had an entrance at first-floor level to allow access without having to pass through the solar.

Although this range of buildings gave the owner a high degree of comfort and was an indication of his wealth and prestige, its thick stone walls and arrow loops – rather than windows – at ground-floor level equipped it to serve in addition as a defensive stronghold.

Below: The solar, showing the central uprights of the crown-post roof

Facing page: View from the solar into the chapel

1 mile E
of Plaxtol
*OS Map 179,
refTR 228693*
Open
2 Apr–29 Sep:
10am–6pm
Sat–Thu and
bank holidays

37

The most dominant features of this site are the 12th-century towers of the former monastic church, which stand out on the skyline for miles around. Coastal erosion has brought the edge of the beach to the towers, which act as a navigation marker for shipping. Much of the site has now been lost to the sea.

Two thousand years ago the geography of this area was very different. The Wantsum, a sea channel up to 4.8km (3 miles) wide, cut off the Isle of Thanet from the mainland, and the Roman fort of Reculver stood on a promontory at the north end of the channel where it joined the Thames estuary. Today the Wantsum has silted up and become dry land.

The imposing towers of the medieval church at Reculver, which still guide ships at sea

History

The Romans conquered Britain under the Emperor Claudius in AD 43. Under Aulus Plautius the Roman armies landed unopposed, but there is debate as to the location of the invasion. A strong candidate is the Wantsum channel, and parts of fortifications of the Claudian period have been found both at Richborough and Reculver, located at opposite ends of the Wantsum. Both sites played a role in the earliest years of the conquest.

During the 1st and 2nd centuries a Roman settlement grew up at Reculver, probably around a harbour. The size of this settlement is unknown as coastal erosion has

destroyed much of the evidence.

In the early 3rd century a fort was built. This was nearly square, with rounded corners, and measured 180m by 175m (590ft by 574ft). Its flint walls were backed with earth ramparts and surrounded by two ditches 10m (33ft) wide. This was one of the very earliest of the forts of the Saxon Shore, built against Saxon raids, and was traditional in its plan. Later Saxon Shore forts (Richborough, Pevensey, Portchester) were built to a new model with projecting bastions. The walls and two of the four gates (south and east) can be seen.

By the 5th century the Romans had abandoned their defence of Britain and the fort at Reculver had fallen into disuse. An Anglo-Saxon monastery was founded on the site in 669, reusing the existing defences, and the church of St Mary was built near the centre of the earlier fort. Documentary evidence suggests that the site had ceased to function as a monastic house by the 10th century, after which time the church became the parish church of Reculver.

Remodelling of the church in the 12th century included the addition of tall twin towers. The medieval church was partly demolished in 1805, when much of the stone was reused to construct a new church on higher ground at Hillborough, but the twin towers were left. They were bought, repaired and underpinned by Trinity House in 1809.

Reculver Abbey, in an 18th-century engraving by Samuel and Nathaniel Buck

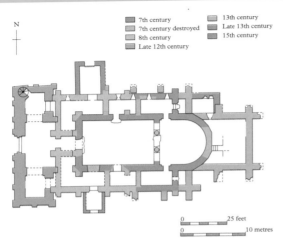

7th century
7th century destroyed
8th century
Late 12th century
13th century
Late 13th century
15th century

N

0   25 feet
0   10 metres

*Plan of the church
at Reculver*

At Reculver
3 miles E of
Herne Bay.
External viewing
only
OS Map 179,
ref TR 228693

Description

The southern half of the Roman fort at Reculver survives as ruined walls and earthworks. The core of the enclosing wall, which would originally have been topped with a wall walk and parapet, is mainly flint and in parts survives to a height of almost 3m (10ft). It can be best appreciated by walking around the outer perimeter of the fort. It was originally faced with squared greensand blocks, but these have almost all disappeared.

There were originally four gateway entrances – one through the centre of each side of the defences. Roughly in the centre of the east wall was the east gate, which consisted of a single carriageway 2.7m (9ft) wide contained within a masonry arch and with a single guard chamber to the north. Tiles in the walls enclosing the guard chamber may represent a later rebuilding. The south gate in the middle of the south wall was of similar form.

Several buildings from the interior of the fort are known, including barracks, a bath-house and the headquarters building. No traces of these buildings, however, remain above ground.

The earliest monastic church on the site, founded in the 7th century, survives in the form of buried foundations, which are marked out in modern concrete, and as standing ruins incorporated in the later parish church. The early walling incorporated reused Roman tiles, bricks and rubble masonry.

Richborough is a key site in the history of Roman Britain, used during the entire length of the occupation from the invasion of AD 43 until the end of Roman rule in 410. It developed from an early fortification to a civilian town and port before returning to military use with the building of a Saxon Shore fort as a protection against Saxon raiders. It has been suggested that the amphitheatre was constructed in the late 3rd century. It provided the inhabitants of the town with a place for entertainments such as wild animal hunts and gladiatorial combat. Romano-British amphitheatres were usually not elaborate structures. Excavations in 1849 and recent geophysical survey of the area indicate an arena surrounded by sloping banks of mixed clay and mortar, which would probably have been used as a support for wooden seats. At the narrow ends of the elliptical plan there are two obvious entrances, while on the north-west and south-east sides there are indications of additional entrances or architectural features, possibly towers.

Today the amphitheatre survives as an elliptical hollow measuring 60m by 50m (197ft by 164ft), which represents the central arena. It is surrounded by a bank 12m (39ft) wide and rising to a height of about 2m (7ft).

Aerial view of Richborough Roman Amphitheatre, to the left of the fort

1¼ miles N of Sandwich off A257; junction 7 of M2, on to A2. Access across grazed land from footpath: from end of access lane to Roman fort turn S for 250m to pick up footpath heading W. Ascend to crest of hill. Amphitheatre is to the right.
OS Map 179, ref TR 324602

ST AUGUSTINE'S CROSS

St Augustine's Cross stands close to the site at which an important meeting between St Augustine and King Ethelbert is said to have taken place nearly 1,500 years ago.

Right: The intricately carved St Augustine's Cross, near Minster

History

The cross was commissioned in 1884 by Granville George Leveson-Gower, second Earl Granville, at the time Minister for Foreign Affairs and Lord Warden of the Cinque Ports. He was inspired to erect it after hearing the story of a massive oak tree felled within living memory and known as the Augustine Oak, one of a group of trees fringing a field which he owned. According to local legend, under

this oak in AD 597 the first meeting was held between King Ethelbert and the monk Augustine, newly arrived from Rome. Augustine had recently landed on the Isle of Thanet, having been sent by Pope Gregory to convert the Anglo-Saxons to Christianity and thereby re-establish the faith in a country in which it had faded with the fall of the Roman Empire.

Not far to the south-east was the stream in which, the legend tells us, Augustine baptised his first convert and which subsequently became known as St Augustine's Well. Tradition holds that Ethelbert was converted to Christianity and Augustine baptised

him on Whit Sunday in AD 597. On Christmas Day of that year, according to a papal letter of AD 598, more than 10,000 baptisms were carried out.

Description

Lord Granville chose to commemorate the meeting between Augustine and Ethelbert with a stone cross in the early Christian style, and as a model he selected the 8th- to 9th-century crosses at Sandbach, near Crewe, Cheshire.

The cross carries carvings illustrating the Christian story on its west side: the Annunciation, the Virgin and Child, the Crucifixion and the Transfiguration. On the north side are the 12 apostles, on the south side 14

early Christian martyrs. The east side has runic ornamentation which continues nearly halfway down the shaft, the design then breaking into panels showing St Alban, St Augustine and Ethelbert. A Latin inscription commemorating the meeting of Ethelbert and Augustine, composed by Dr Liddell, Dean of Christchurch, is carved into the base of the cross. This can be translated as:

After many dangers and difficulties by land and sea Augustine landed at last on the shores of Richborough in the Isle of Thanet. On this spot he met King Ethelbert, and preached his first sermon to our own countrymen. Thus he happily planted the Christian faith, which spread with marvellous speed throughout the whole of England. That the memory of these events may be preserved among the English G G L-G Earl Granville, Lord Warden of the Cinque Ports has erected this monument, AD 1884.

Above: Portrait photograph by Elliott & Fry of Granville George Leveson-Gower

Above left: St Augustine converts King Ethelbert, as depicted in a print by C W Cope

2 miles E of Minster off B29048 OS Map 179, ref TR 340642

This austere building stands alone, surrounded by fields, close to the village of Swingfield. It has undergone many phases of alteration and was restored in the early 1970s.

History

The sisters of the Order of the Knights of St John of Jerusalem had a house at Swingfield until about 1180, when they were removed to Buckland Priory in Somerset. The Knights Hospitaller, of the same order, then established a small community on the site, of which the 13th-century chapel is the only remaining building.

The Knights Hospitaller were a military and religious order founded in the 12th century with the purpose of caring for and protecting pilgrims to the Holy Land. Their main unit of local administration was the commandery, where knights and sergeants lived together under the

St John's Commandery, seen from the east

rule of a commander, who administered the estates with which the order had been endowed. Revenues from commanderies funded hospitals for sick pilgrims.

After the Dissolution of the Monasteries, in 1540 the chapel was converted into a farmhouse, and since then has undergone successive phases of alteration. Traces of other buildings survive only as slight earthworks to the south and west of the chapel.

Description

Although the chapel and part of an adjoining hall were converted into a farmhouse, evidence of the original function of the buildings can still be seen as a result of the 1970s conservation works.

Three lancet windows in the east wall are survivals of the original chapel building and the remarkable crown-post roof may also be part of the 13th-century structure. The chapel has a piscina, or stone basin, where sacred vessels were washed, and an aumbrey, or cupboard, where

the communion vessels were kept. To the east of the south doorway is the consecration cross of the building, carved on the wall.

The two-storey porch on the north wall indicates that the west end of the building always had an upper floor and was once in domestic use. After the Dissolution the building became entirely residential and the interior was converted to accommodate two storeys throughout.

The central chimney stack dates from the 16th century and the ground-floor parlour has a ceiling of the same period with moulded joists and cross-beams. Doors led from this room and from the bedroom above to the south wing, now demolished. There is a pointed-arched opening, dating to the 13th century, to the room above the porch.

The crown-post roof of the chapel

2 miles NE of Densole off A260
OS Map 179, ref TR 232440
External viewing only. Internal viewing by appointment; please call 01304 211067 for details

45

St Leonard's Tower stands on a natural sandstone ledge near the head of a narrow valley on the south-western edge of the village of West Malling.

History

The tower is a mysterious survival. It is thought by some to have been part of a castle built between 1077 and 1108 by Gundulf, Bishop of Rochester, who founded St Mary's Abbey, situated about 700m (760 yds) to the north-east. Alternatively it may have been built by Bishop Odo of Bayeux, who was half-brother of William the Conqueror (and who is thought to have commissioned the famous tapestry); he held church lands at West Malling. The tower takes its name from a chapel dedicated to St Leonard that once stood nearby.

Little is known about the history of St Leonard's Tower. There is no evidence of fireplaces or latrines, which may indicate that the building was used for defensive, rather than domestic, purposes. Alternatively, the tower may have served as a centre for the administration of the local estates of the bishopric. At a later date the roof of the tower was removed and windows were blocked; these alterations may have been related to the building's later use as storage for hops.

St Leonard's Tower viewed from the west

Description

The square tower is constructed of coursed rubble with stone dressings and survives to a height of 20m (66ft). Its walls are 2m (6ft) thick and the building is approximately 10m (33ft) square. It originally contained a basement and two floors, and joist holes which show the level of the wooden floor of the first-floor chamber can still be seen. A spiral staircase in the north-west turret connected the floors.

The original entrance to the tower, through the east face, was reached by a wooden staircase. This was later blocked, and a new round-headed archway was pierced through the western face at ground level. The tower is lit by round-headed windows. Loops through which arrows could be fired to defend the tower can be seen in the turret.

A stretch of medieval walling forming the base of a later garden wall runs from the north-east corner of the tower downhill towards the road. Traces of herringbone stonework indicate that the wall was constructed during the 11th or 12th century and may have formed part of an enclosure attached to the tower. Additional buildings such as stables and workshops were possibly situated within this enclosure.

View of the tower from the south-east

On unclassified road W of A228
OS Map 188, ref TQ 676571
External viewing only. Internal viewing by appointment; please call 01732 870872

The ruin of this medieval castle is situated on the southernmost spur of the Chart Hills, on the eastern edge of the village of Sutton Valence. The castle provides dramatic panoramic views over East Sussex and the Weald of Kent.

History

Sutton Valence was built in the 12th century in order to control the

Sutton Valence Castle seen from the west

important route between Maidstone and the channel ports of Rye and Old Winchelsea.

In the 13th century the castle was part of the Sutton estate and was owned by Simon de Montfort, Earl of Leicester, who led the English barons in revolt against Henry III. After the failure of de Montfort's rising and his death at the battle of Evesham, all of his land was forfeited to the king. Henry granted the Sutton estate to William de Valence, his half-brother, as a reward for his support against the rebels. It then became known as Sutton Valence.

The castle was abandoned in about 1300 and fell into decay. The ruins were conserved in the 1980s.

Description

The tower keep, constructed on a raised terrace, is a square structure built of roughly coursed Kentish ragstone and flint. Its walls, which survive to a height of 7m (23ft), are 11m (36ft) long and more than 2m (7ft) thick. The keep was originally

20m (66ft) high and had timber floors, indicated by joist slots visible in the masonry at first-floor level. Built within the thickness of the southern wall is a barrel-vaulted passage. Traces of the garderobe, or latrine, survive in the south-east angle and can be seen on the outside wall.

Partial excavation in the 1950s showed that the entrance to the keep was situated on the northern side at first-floor level. The entrance was protected by a small masonry building, the foundations of which have been exposed. This was demolished in about 1200 and replaced by a staircase, which was later encased in protective walls. A short length of this walling can be seen north of the keep, surviving to a height of 4m (13ft).

The earthwork defences, which would have formed an enclosure around the keep, have been levelled, and buildings such as stables and workshops, which would have occupied the area within the enclosure, have also disappeared.

5 miles SE of Maidstone in Sutton Valence village on A274
OS Map 188, ref TQ 815491

49

The counties of the South East have been home and inspiration to three notable visual artists of the 20th century. Stanley Spencer was born in Cookham, Berkshire, where he lived and painted for most of his life. His outstanding work, however, is in the Sandham Memorial Chapel at Burghclere in neighbouring Hampshire. This series of murals from 1927, on the subject of the First World War, has been compared in its achievement to Giotto's Arena Chapel in Padua, Italy.

Epsom-born John Piper became known in the 1930s for his romantic portrayal of buildings and places. His interest in Britain's architectural heritage brought him into contact with the poet John Betjeman, and the church near Betjeman's home in Farnborough, Berkshire, has a window dedicated to him by Piper. The stained glass windows in Coventry Cathedral, completed in 1962, are perhaps Piper's most renowned work. The studio of the flamboyant painter Augustus John was near Fordingbridge, in Hampshire, from 1928 until his death in 1961. John is best remembered for his portraits of literary figures such as George Bernard Shaw, Dylan Thomas and Thomas Hardy.

Many writers of classic children's stories lived and worked in the South East. Lewis Carroll was a mathematics lecturer at Christ Church, Oxford, when he befriended the young Alice Liddell, on whom his *Alice's Adventures in Wonderland* (1865) were based; Kenneth Grahame found inspiration for his *The Wind in the Willows* (1908) at Pangbourne,

Above: Self-Portrait, by Stanley Spencer 1923
Right: Photograph of John Piper by Ida Kar

WRITERS AND ARTISTS OF THE SOUTH EAST

Berkshire, where he lived at Church Cottage; and 500 acres of woodland at A A Milne's home in the Ashdown Forest near Hartfield in Sussex became famous as the '100 Acre Wood' in *Winnie the Pooh* (1926). Rudyard Kipling lived for many years at Bateman's, near Burwash, and here he wrote his famous poem 'If'.

Oscar Wilde wrote the *Ballad of Reading Gaol* after his two years of hard labour there; the exploration of how 'each man kills the thing he loves' was one theme of the novel conceived not far away in Marlow, Buckinghamshire. In the same town Mary Shelley completed *Frankenstein*, while living in West Street with her husband, the poet Percy Bysshe Shelley in 1817. In 1887, Jerome K Jerome drew inspiration of a different kind from the same town when writing his humorous novel *Three Men in a Boat*.

From 1856 until his death in 1870, Charles Dickens lived at Gad's Hill Place, near Rochester, spending his summers at Broadstairs. Nearby Cooling churchyard inspired the opening chapter of *Great Expectations* (1860–61).

In contrast to the widely travelled Dickens, the naturalist Gilbert White lived and died in the place he made famous. His *Natural History of Selborne* (1788) celebrates the Hampshire village of that name, where his former home is now a museum.

In 1809 the novelist Jane Austen came to live in a modest brick house in the nearby village of Chawton, where she wrote *Mansfield Park*, *Emma* and *Persuasion*.

Left: *The Shelleys' house in Marlow, photographed by Henry Taunt, 1896*

*Below: View of
Temple Manor from
the north-east*

*Facing page: The
upper chamber with
its inserted
later fireplace*

The stone hall of the manor house of
the Knights Templar is situated to the
west of the River Medway in Strood.
Now surrounded by an industrial
estate, it once stood in farmland,
which in the 13th century provided it
with a substantial income. A leafy
garden now provides a fitting setting
for this fine medieval building.

History

The manor of Strood was given to
the Knights Templar by Henry II in

1159. The Knights Templar was a
military and religious order that was
established at the time of the
Crusades to protect pilgrims
travelling to the Holy Land and to
defend the holy places there.
It acquired extensive possessions in
Europe and became rich and powerful.

Probably no more than two
knights of the order would have lived
permanently at Temple Manor. A
bailiff may have run the estate.

The hall was built about 70 years
after the Templars had acquired the
estate and was designed to provide
suitable lodging for dignitaries
travelling between Dover and
London. A kitchen range and other
service buildings would have been
part of the complex. By the early 14th
century the Templars had converted
the manor into a farm, which was
rented out to tenants.

In 1307 King Philip of France first
seized the possessions of the Templars,
whose wealth and influence had made
them unpopular, and in 1324 the
manor of Strood was formally ceded

to Edward II. In 1336 Edward III gave Temple Manor to the Countess of Pembroke, and the income from it was used to endow an order of Franciscan nuns.

Following the Dissolution of the Monasteries, the property was granted to Edward Elrington in 1539. It passed through many hands and was eventually divided up. In the 1930s the city of Rochester acquired the remaining part of the estate for industrial development. The manor house became derelict and was restored by the Ministry of Works after the Second World War.

Description

The hall is an impressive two-storey flint and stone structure consisting of a first-floor chamber supported by a fine undercroft, or vaulted cellar. Brick extensions were added at each end in the 17th century.

The ornate chamber was used by the knights for both residential and business purposes. The main doorway has Purbeck marble shafts to either

side and complex carved mouldings. The walls are of flint rubble but were originally plastered and painted to simulate smooth stone. The upper floor was reached via an external stair, which was reconstructed in the 1950s. In the 17th century a fireplace was inserted into the chamber at its eastern end.

Archaeological excavation has revealed that a timber hall was added to the north side of this building in the early 14th century and that further buildings were constructed in the 15th century. No trace of these remains today.

Located in Strood (Rochester) off A228 *OS Map 178, ref TQ 733685* Open 1 Apr–30 Sep: 10am–6pm, Sun only; 1–31 Oct: 10am–4pm, Sun only Tel: 01634 338110

Plans to fortify the hills above Dover were drawn up after war broke out with France in 1778. Standing on the Western Heights today, looking at the sweeping views over the town, harbour and castle and, on a fine day, the clear silhouette of the French coast, it is easy to understand why military planners saw the need to embark on this huge project.

The English Heritage properties – which form only a part of the extensive network of fortifications – are situated on the north side of the hill. They include the North Centre Bastion and the Drop Redoubt; 'redoubt' means detached fort, and 'The Drop' was the name formerly given to the area in which it is situated.

In 1779 money was first allocated for fortifications on the Western Heights but it was not until 1781

that the Board of Ordnance bought 33 acres (13 hectares) of land in order to construct the defences first proposed in the 1778 plan – though by the end of the war, in 1783, the works had not been completed. A 1784 map shows a bastioned fort on the site of the present Drop Redoubt and a series of earthwork batteries.

Little further work was carried out until the outbreak of the Napoleonic Wars in 1793. Plans were then drawn up to enhance the existing fortifications: the defences were to consist of a

The Drop Redoubt of the Western Heights, with Dover Castle in the distance

PLEASE NOTE: There is no access to the fortifications at Western Heights and visitors are asked to keep to the footpaths for their own safety

citadel on the west side of the hill and a redoubt on the eastern side, connected by strong defensive lines. The Drop Redoubt was built between 1804 and 1815. Commanding extensive views of the town, harbour and castle, it has barracks for 200 men and was intended to house twelve 24-pounder guns. When the peace treaty with France was signed in 1814 more than £200,000 had been spent on the vast network of fortifications here.

The perceived threat to Britain posed by Napoleon III, Emperor of France, led in 1859 to a review of the state of the nation's fortifications. As a result the northern side of the hill was totally relandscaped and the lines connecting the Drop Redoubt and the citadel were improved. The massive ditches, between 9m (29ft) and 15m (49ft) in depth, were faced with brick. Covering fire from the Drop Redoubt and North Centre Bastion would have allowed the ditches to be swept with artillery and small-arms fire.

The fortifications at the Western Heights, offering sweeping views over the town

During the First World War the Heights were primarily used for barrack accommodation. Gun sites, pillboxes and blast shelters were constructed during the Second World War. The Army finally abandoned the area in stages between 1954 and 1961.

Today there is no access to the fortifications, but it is possible to view the Drop Redoubt and the brick-lined ditches from adjacent footpaths. In parts the defences are overgrown, but it is still possible to gain a good impression of the enormous scale and complexity of this defensive project.

Above Dover town on W side of harbour
OS Map 179, ref TR 312408

WAVERLEY ABBEY

The ruins of Waverley Abbey are situated in a peaceful loop of the River Wey, and still give an impression of the solitude experienced by the monks who founded a monastery here almost 900 years ago.

History

The monastery at Waverley, the first Cistercian house to be established in Britain, was founded by William Gifford, Bishop of Winchester, in 1128. It was colonised with 12 monks and an abbot from Aumone in France. By 1187 there were 70 monks and 120 lay brothers in residence.

In 1201 the abbey buildings were badly flooded. This became a common occurrence and as a result the abbey was substantially rebuilt during the 13th century. It continued to grow in the 14th century. The monks and lay brothers farmed the surrounding land, were active in the Cistercian wool trade and provided shelter for pilgrims and travellers and an infirmary for the sick.

In 1536, with the Dissolution of the Monasteries, the site passed to Sir William Fitzherbert, treasurer of the king's household. Much of the abbey was dismantled and some of the stone was reused to build Sir William More's house at Loseley, a few miles to the east.

Description

Waverley followed the traditional plan of a Cistercian abbey. It featured a large church, almost 91m (300ft) in length. To the south was the chapter house, where the monks would gather

The monks' dormitory at Waverley Abbey, with the lay brothers' quarters beyond

daily to have a chapter of the rule of the order read to them and to discuss business. Further south was the monks' dormitory. The refectory and latrine block lay south of the cloister and the lay brothers' accommodation was situated to the west.

Today only parts, some substantial, of the buildings remain standing, although archaeological excavation has recovered the complete ground plan. The most impressive ruin is that of the lay brothers' quarters, at the far end of the site. The long cellar has graceful columns supporting the vaulting above. Parts of the upper floor and the south wall remain standing. Close by, an end wall and parts of the side walls of the monks' dormitory are visible up to the full height of the gable. To the north are substantial remains of the chapter house and the south transept of the church, as well as traces of the north transept. An isolated stretch of wall to the east of the church is part of the abbey's infirmary chapel.

View of the lay brothers' quarters from the south-west

The monastic precinct covered an area of about 24 hectares (50 acres), bordered to the south and east by the River Wey. The brewhouse and other buildings associated with the economy of the abbey lay in the western part of the precinct – these are visible today only as earthworks. In the eastern part of the precinct are earthwork remains of a water supply system and the fishponds which provided one of the staples of the monks' diet. These remains lie in privately owned meadows and there is no public access to them.

2 miles SE of
Farnham off
B3001 and off
junction 10
of M25
OS Map 186,
ref SU 868453

The remains of Boxgrove Priory stand at the end of a gravel track in a beautiful setting in the village of Boxgrove, at the foot of the South Downs.

History

The Benedictine priory of St Mary the Virgin and St Blaise was founded in about 1117 by Robert de la Haye, Lord of Halnaker. It was a cell of the abbey at Lessay in Normandy in France and, when founded, had a community of only three monks. In 1149 Roger St John increased the number of monks but the priory remained a cell of the French abbey. In 1339, when other alien monastic properties were seized by Edward III, Boxgrove became independent. Following the Dissolution of the Monasteries the buildings and land were granted to Sir Thomas West, Baron de la Warr.

Below: The lodging house of Boxgrove Priory from the east

Description

Of the monastic buildings only the lodging house and part of the church and chapter house remain. They are grouped around a small field, which is the site of the cloister of the monastery.

At the northern edge of the site the ruin of the 14th-century lodging house stands alone. It is roofless, but the north and south gable ends still stand to their full height. The building originally had two storeys, with an undercroft, or vaulted cellar, used for storage. The support for the vault of the undercroft can be seen clearly at the north end of the building.

The west part of the monastic church was demolished in the 18th century but the chancel, central tower, transepts and easternmost bay of the nave survive as the impressive present-day parish church. (This

building is not in the guardianship of English Heritage.) There is a model of the monastic buildings inside the church, as an aid to understanding the layout of the monastery.

Above: The lodging house from the south-west

Left: The parish church of Boxgrove, adjoining the ruins

The north wall of the nave forms part of the wall of the churchyard, and the footings of the south wall and one bay of the south arcade from the interior of the church can also be seen in the churchyard.

One wall of the chapter house, where the monks would have gathered daily to have a chapter of the rule of St Benedict read to them and to discuss business, is attached to the north transept of the church. It has a central doorway with a window to either side.

The remaining monastery buildings lay to the north of the church, surrounding the cloister, but do not survive above ground.

N of Boxgrove, 4 miles E of Chichester on minor road off A27 OS Map 197, ref SU 908076

Bramber Castle stands on the edge of the village of Bramber, on a high natural knoll overlooking the River Adur.

History

Below: The approach to Bramber Castle, with the remains of the gatehouse on the right

Bramber Castle was founded by William de Braose as a defensive and administrative centre for Bramber, one of the six administrative regions –

each of which was controlled by a castle – into which Sussex was divided following the Norman Conquest. It was held almost continually by de Braose and his descendants from its foundation by 1073 until 1450.

One of these descendants, another William de Braose, was among those barons suspected of disloyalty to King John in the early 13th century. The king demanded William's two sons as hostages. Lady de Braose refused, saying she would not trust her sons to a man who had already murdered his own nephew. The castle was confiscated by the king and the family captured. Lady de Braose and her two sons died of starvation while imprisoned at Windsor Castle. King John held Bramber Castle only briefly but is known to have carried out repairs to the buildings. Later the castle passed back to the de Braose family, who held it until the 14th century, and then to the Mowbray family.

Subsidence on a large scale led to the ruin of the castle during the 16th century. Its masonry was later used for building roads in the area, and it may have been occupied briefly by Parliamentarian forces during the Civil War.

Description

The original construction of the castle was centred on a high knoll, on which was built a motte 9m (30ft) high using material quarried from an encircling ditch. The motte is visible as a tree-covered mound in the centre of the site. It was surrounded by a wide bailey, or enclosure, entered on the south side through a stone gatehouse (close to the present entrance to the site). The motte, which probably held a wooden structure, was soon abandoned in favour of a three-storey stone keep and the ditch around the motte was filled in. Only one wall of the keep still stands to a height of 14m. The floor levels within the keep are indicated by joist slots in the masonry. Excavation in 1966 and 1967 revealed that the area north of the gatehouse was built up with clay and

chalk and that a series of buildings were erected in this area. A kitchen lay to the west. The area was used as a rubbish dump in the 14th century, when the buildings east of the motte may have become the main accommodation. The lower courses of these structures can still be seen.

An outer ditch was dug around the knoll and an outer bank created to strengthen the defences, probably at the same time as the keep was built. The wall around the top of the knoll was renewed in stone, and parts of this impressive construction still stand to a height of 3m (10ft).

Above: The defensive ditch surrounding the motte and bailey

Left: View from the castle over the Sussex countryside

On W side of Bramber village, off A283
OS Map 198, ref TQ 187107

HAMPSHIRE & THE ISLE OF WIGHT

Hampshire and the Isle of Wight, in the centre of southern England, formed one county until relatively recently. The region features a remarkably diverse landscape: including the distinctive heathlands of the New Forest – the hunting ground of Norman kings – the tree-crowned chalk downlands, the fine trout streams and the spectacular Needles on the coast of the Isle of Wight.

Evidence of prehistoric settlement can be found in the burial mounds constructed at Littleton 4,000 years ago, among other examples. The legacy of Roman occupation can still be found in the remains at Silchester, among other sites.

Numerous fortifications over the centuries were built to protect sea passages in the Solent and important harbours at Portsmouth and Southampton, which developed respectively as major naval centre and international passenger port. One of the most significant fortifications is the Norman castle at Portchester, built within the walls of a Roman fort, while Hurst and Calshot castles were two of a series of coastal forts constructed by Henry VIII. Among later monuments, The Grange at Northington is one of the early Greek Revival houses in Europe, while the Italianate Osborne House famously became the summer home of Queen Victoria and Prince Albert.

Right: The Needles, on the Isle of Wight coast

FLOWERDOWN BARROWS

On the edge of the village of Littleton, this tranquil site contains three prehistoric round barrows. These are burial mounds constructed in the early Bronze Age, 4,000 years ago. The barrows here, originally part of a larger group, stand on a ridge and may have acted as territorial markers. This group is a particularly important prehistoric monument as it survives so well. A large proportion, almost 75 per cent, of Hampshire barrows have been destroyed or badly damaged by development or ploughing, and only 5 per cent survive intact. Round barrows took various forms: the group at Flowerdown includes a disc barrow and two bowl barrows. Bowl barrows, the most numerous surviving form, consisted of a mound of turf, soil or rock, covering one or more burials, and usually surrounded by a circular ditch from which the mound material may have been quarried. Funerary ceremonies and rituals may have taken place on the site for some time before the mound was constructed and the

Flowerdown Barrows, seen from the south

burials sealed. The burials were either inhumations, where a crouched body lying on its side was buried in a small pit, or cremations, where ashes, which were often contained in an urn, were placed in the ground. Grave goods are occasionally found with these burials. Such items included pottery vessels containing food and drink, and weapons, flint tools and pieces of jewellery, to accompany the dead person in the afterlife.

Disc barrows are rare and are particularly likely to have been damaged as they are relatively low earthworks. Many survive only as crop-marks on cultivated land. A disc barrow was constructed as a circular area of level ground surrounded by a ditch and an external bank, with one or more small low mounds covering burials within the central platform. These burials, usually cremations, were frequently accompanied by vessels, tools and personal ornaments. The individuals were probably of high status, as excavated examples contain rich grave goods.

The disc barrow lies at the north end of the site. It has a circular, flat platform 28m (92ft) in diameter, on which lie two low circular mounds. The platform is bounded by a wide ditch and an external bank. To the south-west the larger of the two bowl barrows is 20m (66ft) in diameter and 1m (3ft) high, with a central hollow. The smaller bowl barrow lies close to the outer edge of the disc barrow bank and has a low, roughly circular mound 8m (26ft) in diameter and 0.3m (1ft) high.

Although the barrows may have been disturbed in the past, possibly by 19th-century antiquarians who left no record of their excavations, they undoubtedly provide information about the lives of our Bronze Age ancestors. The barrows contain the Bronze Age land surface, which contains valuable environmental evidence, such as seeds and molluscs, from which the modern archaeologist can build up a picture of the vegetation, climate and farming practices of the past.

Off B3049 out of Winchester to Littleton. Opposite post office in Littleton village OS Map 185, ref SU 459320

KING JAMES'S GATE AND LANDPORT GATE

Below right: The imposing arches of King James's Gate

Far right: The Landport Gate with its fine octagonal turret

King James's Gate forms the officers' entrance to the United Services Recreation Ground on Burnaby Road; Landport Gate is the men's entrance on St George's Road

OS Map 196
King James's Gate ref SZ 636999
Landport Gate ref SZ 634998

The strategic position of Portsmouth and its vital importance for the defence of the Channel coast led to the development of a protective circuit of defences around the town. Earthen ramparts constructed in the 14th century were strengthened by Henry VIII, and in 1665 Charles II instituted a major programme of reconstruction of the defences, and the building of the four gateways.

King James's Gate

King James's Gate was constructed in 1687. It was originally situated in Broad Street, in the south-west part of the town, close to the seaward defences, which still stand. The

gateway was dismantled in 1860 and was re-erected in its present position in the early 20th century. Constructed of brick with stone facing, it has a tall arched opening with flanking pilasters and smaller arches, with 20th-century panelled doors.

Landport Gate

The Landport Gate provided the main entrance to fortified Portsmouth and is the only gateway to survive on its original site. The design of the gate has been attributed to Nicholas Hawksmoor, though it was constructed in 1760 after his

death. It features a simple stone arch surmounted by a fine octagonal turret. While built primarily for defensive purposes, these elegant town gates stand also as testimony to civic pride, and are rare survivors from this period.

The ruins of the Cistercian abbey of St Mary of Edwardstow stand close to Southampton Water, now almost completely surrounded by later development. In their leafy setting, however, they convey the atmosphere of the austere and ordered lives of the monks who once occupied the site.

History

The abbey was founded in 1239 by the Bishop of Winchester, Peter des Roches, and was settled by monks from Beaulieu, also in Hampshire. Henry III assumed patronage in 1251, and this may account for the particular grandeur of the church, where his name appears on the base of a pillar.

Despite royal involvement Netley remained a relatively poor house and was in decline even before the Reformation. In 1536, following the Dissolution of the Monasteries, it was granted to Sir William Paulet, who converted it into an impressive house in which Elizabeth I is known to have stayed.

By 1700 the house had fallen out of use, however, and parts were sold, dismantled, or demolished and removed. Material from the abbey was used in the rebuilding of St Mary's Church, Southampton, and fragments of the north transept of the church were incorporated into a folly built in the grounds of Cranbury Park, near Winchester. Most of the Tudor additions were removed, leaving the monastic ruins much as they appear today. The neglected site became overgrown with trees and ivy. It

Below: The ruins of Netley Abbey, showing the presbytery from the west

Above: *Aerial view of Netley Abbey, looking south-west*

Facing page: *Plan of Netley Abbey*

attracted the attention of writers and poets, including Horace Walpole and Thomas Gray, and artists such as J M W Turner and John Constable. Jane Austen visited the site, which was by the early 19th century well known as a romantic Gothic ruin.

Description

Netley Abbey was built to the typical Cistercian monastic plan, with a church connected to a cloister around which the monks' living quarters were arranged.

The ruins of the roofless church

still give a good impression of its original size and appearance. The north transept has been removed but the south transept stands to roof level. A door from the south transept leads into the still-roofed sacristy, where the priests' vestments and sacred vessels used in the Mass were kept.

In the Tudor conversion the church became the great hall, and an adjacent kitchen was constructed. Tudor brickwork can be seen at the top of the south wall, and a doorway leading into the church from the cloister to the south also dates from this period. The choir remained in use as a family chapel and the south transept became the family's private quarters.

The chapter house, where the monks met daily to have a chapter of the rule of the order read to them and to discuss business, lies to the south of the sacristy on the east side of the cloister. Above was the monks' dormitory, and leading from it the latrine block. This structure lies at a slightly different angle to the rest of the monastic buildings so that it discharged into the stream that ran below. Beneath the dormitory was the day room, where there was some relaxation of monastic discipline. Beneath the latrine block is a vaulted room, well preserved, possibly the infirmary. The eastern range was converted into a long gallery in the 16th century, but the outlines of some of the small rectangular windows of the dormitory, which were blocked or replaced by the much larger Tudor ones, can still be seen.

The monks' refectory lay to the south of the cloister on a north–south alignment. This was demolished by Sir William Paulet to make way for the building of a new gatehouse, to form a grand entrance to his house. The south range of the ruin has brickwork, a doorway and windows, all typical of the Tudor period. On the north wall of this range can be seen the lavatorium, where the monks would have washed before meals. The cloister became Sir William's inner courtyard, with a fountain in the centre. Little remains of the west range, which in the Cistercian plan usually provided accommodation for the lay brothers. To the east of the abbey is a separate building, thought to have been the abbot's lodgings, and the outline of the Tudor garden, which occupied the area between this building and the main abbey.

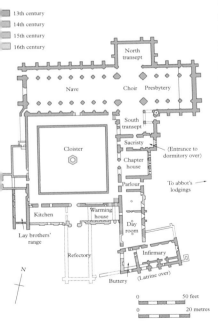

13th century
14th century
15th century
16th century

North transept
Nave
Choir Presbytery
South transept
Sacristy
Cloister
Chapter house
Parlour
(Entrance to dormitory over)
To abbot's lodgings
Kitchen
Warming house
Day room
Lay brothers' range
Refectory
Infirmary
Buttery
(Latrine over)

N

0   50 feet
0   20 metres

In Netley,
4 miles SE
of Southampton,
facing
Southampton
Water
OS Map 196,
ref SU 453090

Below: The portico at the east end of Northington Grange

Facing page: The steps leading up to the east front of the orangery

In the heart of the Hampshire countryside, reached along a farm track, stands The Grange, Northington, a large neoclassical mansion in the form of a Greek temple, one of the finest examples of this type of architecture in Europe.

The lands forming the present estate were held by Hyde Abbey (in Winchester) in the 14th century. In 1538, after the Dissolution of the

Monasteries, they passed to the Crown, and were eventually acquired in 1662 by Sir Robert Henley, a successful lawyer. He commissioned a house from the architect William Samwell, who was a follower of Inigo Jones, the architect who introduced the Palladian style to Britain. The 17th-century west front has recently been restored to its original appearance, following the demolition of 19th-century additions; the rest of Samwell's work is encased within the present building.

In 1761 Robert Henley, a descendant of the first Sir Robert and ennobled in 1764 as the first Lord Northington, employed Robert Adam to design a kitchen block and a bridge. He also laid out the park landscape and created lakes by damming the river.

The exterior of the rest of the building (apart from the west front) is as remodelled between 1809 and 1816 by the owner at the time, Henry Drummond. The architect of this phase was William Wilkins, who had just returned from a study tour of Greek archaeological sites. Architects working in the neoclassical style were already experimenting with ancient Greek sources, and Drummond wished to outdo his neighbour, Sir Francis Baring, who had commissioned George Dance to remodel Stratton Park. Wilkins completely remodelled

the exterior in the form of a Greek temple with a magnificent Doric portico at the east end, but Drummond soon lost interest and sold the property to Alexander Baring.

In 1818 Baring commissioned a western extension – which has since been demolished – from Sir Robert Smirke. The only surviving addition from this period is the neoclassical conservatory created between 1823 and 1825 by the architect Charles Robert Cockerell. This was converted into a picture gallery in about 1880.

The Grange and its estate were sold in 1933. The buildings were occupied by the Army during the Second World War. In 1964 John Baring bought back the estate for the Baring family to farm, and in 1969 planning permission was obtained to demolish the now empty house. Public outcry saved the main building and in 1975 the house, the picture gallery and a small area of pleasure ground passed into the guardianship of the state. The roof was repaired to make the building watertight and the 17th-century west front was restored.

The house now provides a venue for the performance of opera: the picture gallery has been converted and a new auditorium has been sunk into the ground.

Exterior viewing only. 4 miles N of New Alresford, off B3046 along a farm track for 450m (493 yds) *OS Map 185, ref SU 562362* Open 31 Mar–31 May: 10am–6pm; 1 Jun–31 Jul: 10am–3pm; 1 Aug–30 Sep: 10am–6pm; 1 Nov–31 Mar: 10am–4pm Closes 3pm June and July for opera evenings. Tel: 01424 775705

Below: The Royal
Garrison Church seen
from the south-west

Facing page: The
stained-glass windows
in the church, which
serve as a memorial
to the soldiers of
the garrison

Medieval hospital, Tudor ammunition store and church for the Forces since the 1580s, the Royal Garrison Church has stood in Portsmouth for nearly 800 years.

History

The church was founded in about 1212 by Peter des Roches, Bishop of Winchester, as part of a complex of buildings serving as a hostel for pilgrims and a hospital for the sick and elderly. It consisted of an aisled hall (now the ruined nave) and a chapel behind a wall in the east end

(the surviving chancel). Medieval hospitals placed the beds in bays in the aisles within sight of the chapel.

In 1540, after the Reformation, the building was used as an ammunition store, and it started to decay. In 1559 the great Elizabethan project to build up the defences at Portsmouth began. The medieval hospital became part of the governor's house, where two significant events in the history of the site took place. These were the marriage of Charles II to Catherine of Braganza in 1662 and the grand receptions held in 1814 to celebrate

the defeat of Napoleon, attended by the Prince Regent, the Emperor of Russia, the King of Prussia and his general Marshall Blücher, the great ally of Arthur Wellesley, first Duke of Wellington.

In the 19th century the architect G E Street was responsible for a 10-year refurbishment and repair programme of the church, including a new south porch and vestry, new flooring, and specially designed furnishings and memorial windows. This was completed by 1871, and the church took on a 13th-century appearance that it had not presented for many centuries.

In 1933 the church came into the care of the Office of Works, but a firebomb raid in 1941 destroyed the nave. The nave ruins now stand divided from the intact chancel by a modern screen wall.

Description

In plan the church consists of a nave with north and south aisles, and the south porch. The chancel consists of the choir and sanctuary. The choir has two south doors, one of which leads to the stairs up to the bell turret, and the other to the exterior. To the north is the vestry.

The thick lower section of the south wall is part of the original construction. Above this there are three restored lancet windows and a series of corbels serving as beam supports. The south porch and the west wall were both built in the 1860s, as the church had been shortened by one bay in the 1580s.

The chancel features an elaborate vaulted roof with decorative bosses. The east window of three lancets with a trefoiled head is an original feature and inspired Street's restoration of the other windows.

The oak stalls of the 1870s are dedicated as memorials to the nation's most famous sailors and soldiers, beginning with Horatio Nelson and the Duke of Wellington.

Grand Parade, Portsmouth
OS Map 196, ref SZ 633992
Open 1 Apr–30 Sep: 11am–4pm
Mon–Sat

MEDIEVAL COASTAL DEFENCES

The coastline from the Solent to the Thames estuary has always been Great Britain's front door to invaders, and as a consequence has been one of the most heavily defended parts of the country. This can be seen, for example, in the layers of defences built from the Iron Age onwards on the site of Dover Castle: the sea crossing between Dover and France is the shortest between the British Isles and the Continent.

Successive invading forces have landed in this area, most notably the Romans and the Normans, and all strengthened their gains with fortresses. Both the Romans and the Normans initially built with timber and earth but, as time went on and their gains were consolidated, many forts and castles were rebuilt in stone. New medieval keeps were built at Portchester, Hastings, Dover and Rochester. The castles at Portchester and Pevensey are all the more remarkable as they were constructed within, and reused, the walls of pre-existing Roman forts. The main function of these early castles was to control the surrounding countryside by the use of mobile groups of armed men and knights.

The development of the castle as a means of defence became progressively more sophisticated and, from the 13th century, the gradual introduction of

Portchester Castle, Hampshire

Deal Castle, Kent

gunpowder, both as an explosive and as a propellant for artillery, started to influence its design. Initially the battering action of the early 'bombards' was comparable in effect to the existing stone-throwing siege machines. It was the gradual introduction of handguns during the 14th century that brought about more obvious changes, and the evidence of their use can be seen in the form of gun ports at the town gates of Southampton, Winchester and Canterbury, and at Cooling and Bodiam castles.

During the 15th century artillery became ever more powerful, but the new castles – like the magnificent Herstmonceux Castle, in Sussex – were grand houses built to impress, and would have had only limited ability to withstand a well-prepared assault. Work on building functional artillery fortifications did not begin until about 1538, when Henry VIII embarked on an anti-invasion scheme, constructing blockhouses and forts along the British coast from the Humber to Milford Haven in west Wales. In the South East these defences were built at several locations, from

Hurst Castle in Hampshire, round to Milton Blockhouse, Gravesend, Kent. They marked a substantial shift in the method of coastal defence, as the use of artillery enabled the defenders to prevent ships coming close inshore and landing an invasion force. These structures were intended from the outset to be occupied by the military only, and were designed to both mount and resist artillery. Their main characteristics were a compact plan, tiered artillery positions giving interlocking fields of fire, thick masonry walls with rounded shot-deflecting parapets, substantial screening by an earthen glacis, or rampart, and a dry moat. Among the finest built are those at Camber, Deal, Sandown, Sandgate and Walmer.

Above: Camber Castle, East Sussex, one of
Henry VIII's Channel forts
Left: A pile of catapult stones
at Pevensey Castle, East Sussex

The remains of the Roman town of Calleva Atrebatum lie at Silchester in the north Hampshire countryside. Today this peaceful rural site gives visitors the opportunity to appreciate the size and importance of the large, vibrant Roman town that once flourished here. In its heyday Calleva was an economic, cultural and administrative centre for the region, with a regular grid of streets, fine public buildings, houses, shops and workshops. The walls, some of the best-preserved Roman town defences in England, and remains of the amphitheatre still stand.

The remains of the north gate of the Roman town at Silchester

History

The history of Silchester does not, however, begin with the arrival of the Romans. In the pre-Roman Iron Age it was the site of an *oppidum*, a nucleated settlement of the local tribal group, the Atrebates; the name adopted by the Romans, Calleva Atrebatum, can be translated as the 'town of the Atrebates in the woods'. Evidence from archaeological excavations suggests that there were two main phases of occupation in the Iron Age. The first settlement consisted of a cluster of wooden roundhouses, but towards the end of the 1st century BC this was replaced by a more formal, regular arrangement of streets at right angles to one another. The densely occupied settlement was protected by earthwork banks and ditches.

The Atrebates had close links with the Roman Empire and imported fine pottery, amphorae containing wine and olive oil, and other luxury goods. Evidence of a Roman lifestyle, such as implements for writing in Latin and foods such as oysters, indicates this close relationship. In return the Atrebates exported corn, slaves, hides and hunting dogs to Rome. Coins bear the mark CALLE and were probably minted in Calleva.

The settlement may have been briefly abandoned before Roman rebuilding started in about AD 50. In this area of Britain a peaceful transition from client kingdom (an alliance between native tribes and Rome) to Roman-occupied province took place.

The Roman town was laid out on a newly orientated street grid. The forum and basilica, occupying a large central site, were the focus of the town. The forum, enclosed on three sides by shops and offices and on the fourth, western, side by the basilica, provided an open space for public meetings and markets. The basilica contained the council chamber, court and administrative offices of the town. Built originally of timber, it was rebuilt in stone in the mid-2nd century AD. Other public buildings included the baths in the south-east part of the town and a large inn near the south gate for travellers on official business. The baths were sited beside a spring-fed stream but the water supply may have been augmented by water piped from further afield. Several Romano-Celtic temples and shrines were built and an amphitheatre was constructed to the north-east of the town. The remaining buildings, including shops, workshops and houses, ranged from small, undivided structures to large

Reconstruction drawing of a possible Christian church at Silchester in the 4th century, with the forum and basilica behind

buildings set around courtyards. They were of stone or timber-framed construction, with stone foundations and roofed with sandstone or limestone slabs. The principal rooms had decorated plaster walls and sometimes mosaic or tiled floors and under-floor heating. Many windows were glazed.

Towards the end of the 2nd century AD a defensive circuit was built around the town. This consisted of a rampart and ditches with elaborate masonry gates. It was strengthened in about AD 270 by the addition of a wall to the front of the rampart.

The end of Roman Calleva is obscure. A few isolated finds suggest that the town was occupied until about the 5th century but thereafter it appears to have been deserted. The threat represented by early Saxon settlements not far to the north at Dorchester-on-Thames and to the south at Winchester may have led to the town's abandonment. No evidence of destruction has been found and the town's decay may have been the result of a gradual loss of surrounding territory. The Roman town gradually reverted to open country.

Description

Most Roman towns in Britain were subsequently occupied and developed and as a result the record of Roman life was obscured or destroyed. This is not the case at Silchester. There are no visible remains of the streets and buildings within the town but the stone-built foundations, roads and

The distinctive shape of the Roman town at Silchester, still visible from the air

other features survive intact beneath the surface. Excavations between 1890 and 1909 revealed a complete ground plan of the town, while recent and ongoing excavations by the University of Reading, which use techniques unknown to the Victorians, are revealing the complex multi-phased history of Calleva.

The path from the car park to the north-west of the town follows the course of part of the pre-Roman defensive bank and ditch, and leads to the west gate. The Roman town wall survives as a complete circuit 2.5km (1.5 miles) long, forming a nine-sided enclosure of 43 hectares (107 acres). The wall stands up to 4.5m (15ft) high and 3m (10ft) thick at the base. It is built of flint quarried from the local chalk, with binding courses of flat stone slabs. The original facing was of dressed flint but little of this survives. Remains of the north and south gates can also be seen. In the south-west part of the circuit the outer ditch, which would originally have encircled the walls, is visible.

To the north-east of the town are the remains of the amphitheatre. It was probably first built in about AD 50 and was modified in the early 2nd and 3rd centuries. Earth banks, supported first by timber, then by stone revetments of which the lower courses can still be seen, were constructed around the arena, which was oval in plan. Timber terracing and seating provided space for between 4,500 and 9,000 spectators. It is likely that the crowds were entertained by wild animal hunts and gladiatorial combat.

Silchester, with the amphitheatre outside its walls, as it might have looked in the late 3rd or 4th century

On a minor road, 1 mile E of Silchester
OS Map 175, ref SU 643624

*Right: The remains
of the priory
at Southwick*

Southwick Priory is set in quiet woodland in southern Hampshire.

History

The Augustinian priory was founded by Henry I in 1133, within the walls of Portchester Castle. The priory church is still in use as the parish church of Portchester. During the civil wars between King Stephen and his cousin Matilda the canons complained that the language and rough behaviour of the soldiers in the castle interfered with their religious practices. In 1145 the priory was moved to a quieter location in the countryside at Southwick.

With the Dissolution of the Monasteries, in 1538 the priory was granted to Thomas White, an ally of Thomas Wriothesley who acquired Titchfield Abbey (see pp. 82–3) at the same time. Some of the buildings were reused and modified into a house, but this burnt down in 1750 and a new house was constructed to the north of the priory site.

Description

Today only a short length of the north wall of the priory's refectory survives. Surrounding it are the buried foundations of the medieval and Tudor buildings. Although only a small fragment of the medieval building, the wall tells part of the story of Southwick's history.

The lower section has a series of pillars which supported the vaulting of the undercroft, or cellar. Blocked

arched windows above relate to the early priory building, while the square windows and red brickwork show the type of modification that was made to convert the priory into a house.

In the 1980s a sculpted frieze of the highest quality was found concealed behind a brick wall. It is believed to be a part of the monks' lavatorium, where they would have washed before meals.

Left: A scalloped capital on one of the wall shafts

Below: A drawing of the fine sculpted frieze found in the 1980s, which was possibly part of the monks' lavatorium

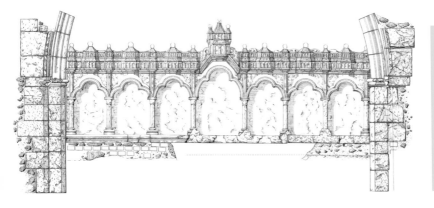

On SE edge of Southwick village, off A333
OS Map 196, ref SU 628084
No public access.
For more information call
01424 775705

Below: The imposing Tudor gatehouse at Titchfield Abbey

Facing page: Some of the surviving medieval tiles of the cloister floor

The ruins of Titchfield Abbey are situated in the valley of the River Meon in south Hampshire.

History

The abbey of St Mary and St John the Evangelist was founded in 1232 by Peter des Roches, Bishop of Winchester, for Premonstratensian canons, an order founded at Prémontré in France and known also as the 'White Canons'.

The abbey owned many thousands of acres of land and had its own farm buildings and a series of fishponds. Titchfield was a good stopping-off place for journeys to the Continent, and Henry V stayed there before going on campaign in France.

At the Dissolution of the Monasteries, the estate passed in 1537 to Thomas Wriothesley, first Earl of Southampton. By 1542 he had converted the monastic buildings into the residence known as Place House. Royal guests to the house included Edward VI, Elizabeth I and Charles I with his queen, Henrietta Maria. The third Earl of Southampton was a patron of William Shakespeare and it is believed that some of Shakespeare's plays were performed here for the first time. Place House survived until 1781, when most of the building was demolished for building stone.

In the early 20th century archaeological excavations helped to clarify the layout of the monastic buildings, and the abbey plan is marked out on the ground.

Description

The abbey was built to the usual monastic plan around a quadrangular cloister. At Titchfield the cloister lay to the north of the church and was surrounded by the chapter house, dormitory, kitchen and, opposite the church, the refectory.

Little remains of the monastic buildings and the site is now dominated by the gatehouse of the Tudor mansion, built into the nave of the church between 1537 and 1542. The gatehouse towers have large turrets, gargoyles on the parapets and mock arrow slits on the ground floor. The original fine wooden doors remain. Inside the nave of the church the 16th-century floor levels can be identified by the position of the fireplaces. All the original church windows were filled and square-headed mullioned windows inserted in their place. Much of the west end of the church was rebuilt in Tudor brick and there are elaborate Tudor chimneys. A few internal details of the original church interior can be seen, including

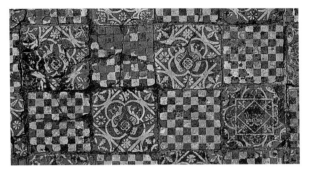

a shaft in the south-west corner of the building which supported the vaulting, and part of a spiral staircase in the west corner turret.

The former entrance to the chapter house, where the monks met daily to hear a reading of a chapter of the rule of the order and to discuss business, can still be seen in the much-altered facade of the east range. The doorway is framed internally by elegant columns of Purbeck marble. Medieval floor tiles survive in the cloister, which became the courtyard of the Tudor mansion. The west range is entirely Tudor. The site is enclosed by a 16th-century boundary wall.

½ mile N of
Titchfield,
off A27
OS Map 196,
ref SU 542067
Open 1 Apr–30
Sep: 10am–6pm;
1–31 Oct:
10am–5pm;
1 Nov–31 Mar:
10am–4pm
Closed 25 Dec
Tel: 01329
842133

WOLVESEY CASTLE (OLD BISHOP'S PALACE)

Below: The ruins of Wolvesey Castle, seen from the south

Facing page: Painting by E W Hazlehurst of the ruins in 1908

The ruins of Wolvesey Castle, the chief residence of the Bishops of Winchester, stand in the south-east corner of the walled area of the city of Winchester, close to the cathedral.

History

Established in Anglo-Saxon times, the bishop's residence was greatly extended after the Norman Conquest in 1066. The second Norman bishop,

William Gifford, built the west hall in about 1110, but the form of the buildings as they survive today is largely the creation of Henry of Blois. Henry was a grandson of William the Conqueror and younger brother of King Stephen. A vital supporter of his brother in his contest with Matilda, Henry I's daughter and nominated heir, he is said to have been one of the richest churchmen of his time.

While later bishops spent more time at their other houses, Wolvesey continued to be used for ceremonial purposes. From 1302, following a major fire in the royal apartments at Winchester Castle, the monarchs stayed at Wolvesey for state occasions, or when they attended the Winchester parliament or functions at the cathedral. Henry V met French ambassadors here in 1415, when they tried to persuade him to renounce his claim to the French throne.

Wolvesey, Farnham Castle and Winchester Palace at Southwark (see pp. 15–17) remained in the Bishop of Winchester's hands after the

Reformation. The last great state occasion at Wolvesey took place in 1554, when the wedding banquet was held here after the marriage of Mary Tudor to Philip II of Spain.

In the 1680s Bishop George Morley decided to build a new palace on the site, perhaps prompted by Charles II's decision to build a royal palace in the town. The medieval chapel was retained but the moat was filled and the rest of the buildings stripped in order to create a new baroque palace to the south.

By the mid-18th century the bishops preferred Farnham Castle as their main residence and Wolvesey was neglected. In 1785 the baroque palace was demolished, apart from the west wing. This wing sustained a number of changes of use and in 1936 it once again became the bishop's house.

Description

The main entrance to the medieval palace was in roughly the same place as the present entrance from College

WOLVESEY CASTLE (OLD BISHOP'S PALACE)

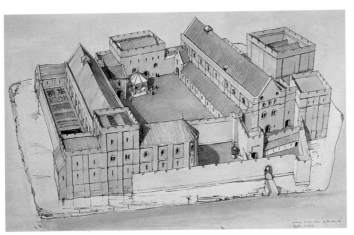

Reconstruction drawing of the west and east halls of Wolvesey Castle, with the chapel in the foreground, in about 1140

chapel, lie under the present bishop's house and garden.

Today the gravelled areas indicate the site of former buildings, while the grassed areas represent outdoor spaces. As the visitor enters the complex of buildings through the modern gateway, the original entrance can be seen to the west as foundations at the base of the more recent wall. A round-headed doorway leads into the east hall. The low walls in front of the doorway are the foundations of a gatehouse and outer defensive building.

The east hall was built as an impressive public room in which the bishop would dine and receive visitors in state. The north and south gable ends survive to a considerable height, but the remainder of the building is represented by low walls and foundations. The hall was built of flint with stone detailing. The walls were

Street. The area now used as playing fields was the site of the outer courtyard and stables, barns, the bishop's prison and the bishop's wool-house, from which the lucrative trade in wool from the bishop's estates was managed.

The palace was arranged around an inner courtyard surrounded by a moat, which was filled in by Bishop Morley and is no longer visible. Parts of the south and west wings of the palace, formerly connected to the

originally rendered and whitewashed. The red tiles are not original but the result of consolidation works carried out in the 1920s.

The hall rose to the full height of the building. A low gallery ran along the west wall, and a porch led into the hall at the north end. At the south end the two rooms either side of the passage into the hall were used as the pantry and buttery, for storing food, wine and beer. On the first floor was the bishop's great chamber.

To the south-east of the hall is a square tower, originally built by Henry of Blois as a latrine tower. Later, during the civil wars of Stephen's reign, it was remodelled.

To the east of the hall is a square roofless building which was probably the kitchen block. This would have been open to the rafters, with huge fireplaces on which food would have been cooked for the bishop and his guests in the hall.

West of the hall is an area laid to grass, once the central courtyard of the palace. To the north, across a passageway linking the west and east halls, is a gatehouse, Woodman's Gate, built by Henry of Blois. A drawbridge could be lowered to cross the moat.

To the west of Woodman's Gate is the site of the earlier west hall. Wooden steps give a view over the surviving walls, but most of the building now lies under the present bishop's house. The hall was constructed by William Gifford in 1116, possibly as an addition to the existing Anglo-Saxon bishop's residence. At the south end was a tower, at least three storeys high, which contained the bishop's exchequer or treasury, private chapel and bedroom. At the north end was a further latrine block added by Henry of Blois; the drains, which emptied into the moat, can still be seen.

Attached to the west hall was Henry of Blois's chapel. The chapel seen today, which is not open to the public, was built in the mid-15th century on the foundations of Henry's chapel. It is now part of the present bishop's residence.

¾ mile SE of Winchester Cathedral, next to the Bishop's Palace; access from College Street

OS Map 185, ref SU 484291

Open 1 Apr–30 Sep: 10am–5pm

St Catherine's Oratory, which is situated on St Catherine's Hill, Isle of Wight, overlooking Chale Bay, is the site of a prehistoric burial mound and a small medieval oratory, or chapel, the west tower of which is thought to have been used as a lighthouse.

History

It is likely that the oratory, completed in 1328, was erected by Walter de Godeton, a local landowner who was condemned by the Church for stealing casks of wine from a shipwreck which had occurred in 1314 off Chale Bay. The ship was one of a fleet carrying a cargo of white wine for the monastery of Livers in Picardy. The Church threatened de Godeton with excommunication unless he built a lighthouse above the scene of the shipwreck, together with an adjoining oratory. The oratory was to be endowed to maintain a priest to tend the light and to say masses for souls lost at sea. The duties were apparently carried out until the Reformation in the 16th century.

Description

The lighthouse tower, known as the Pepperpot, is a four-storey octagonal structure of greensand stone, with a pitched roof of stone tiles on a domed brick vault. Eight windows on the third floor form a lantern. The tower's arched door-heads suggest that it was substantially repaired in the mid-16th century, possibly when anxiety about the threat from the Spanish Armada would have given the building an important role as a lookout tower and beacon site.

The lighthouse, which formed the western tower of St Catherine's Oratory, is all that still stands of the original building. The remains of the walls can still be seen, however, as grass-covered banks forming three sides of a square, with the lighthouse on the west side. The banks are approximately 12m (39ft) apart and in places stand to 1m (3ft) in height. An earth bank 0.5m (1.5ft) high, the turf wall of the churchyard, encloses the oratory site on its north, west and south sides.

At a distance of 15m (49ft) to the south-east of the tower is a much earlier monument, a Bronze Age bowl barrow, or burial mound, which was constructed on this hilltop site about 4,000 years ago. Bowl barrows consisted of a mound of turf, soil or rock, covering one or more burials, and usually surrounded by a circular ditch from which the mound material may have been quarried. This barrow, which is 20m (66ft) in diameter and 2m (6ft) high, was partially excavated in 1925, when human and animal bones and flint tools were discovered. At some time during the medieval period, possibly during the construction of the oratory, a lime kiln was built into the side of the barrow. To the south are pits and mounds which may have resulted from mining chalk to provide lime for the kiln.

St Catherine's Oratory, which commands sweeping views along the coastline of the Isle of Wight

³/₄ mile NW of Niton
OS Map 196, ref SZ 494773

In 1937 an exhibition, 'Modern Architecture in England', was organised by the Museum of Modern Art in New York. It featured not simply recently completed structures, but specifically Modern Movement buildings, almost all of which had been constructed in London or the South East of England. These included the Peter Jones store on Sloane Square, London (by Slater and Moberly, 1936), some of the new suburban Underground stations and many flat-roofed houses (for example, the house at Iver, Buckinghamshire, by F R S Yorke, 1936, and the studio for Augustus John at Fordingbridge, Hampshire, by Christopher Nicholson, 1934). But what was so special about these new buildings?

Modern Movement architects shared a set of aesthetic and social values. They were interested in new technologies and ways of living, in looking to the future – to the impact of machines and mass production – rather than to the historic architecture of the past. In the post-war period they were to have huge influence as Britain built the major housing, school and hospital projects which appealed to their socialist ambitions, but in the 1930s there was little money to build anything beyond relatively modest private houses for adventurous clients and speculative buildings for entertainment and commerce.

The newly championed architects were influenced by developments on the Continent, most notably by the villas of the Swiss-born French architect Le Corbusier.

Above: The main staircase of the De La Warr Pavilion at Bexhill-on-Sea, East Sussex
Right: The De La Warr Pavilion's south front

BUILDINGS OF THE MODERN MOVEMENT

His polemical book *Vers une architecture*, in which he encouraged architects to seek inspiration in the bold forms of grain silos and factories and to study the production of ships and cars, was translated into English in 1927 by the architect Frederick Etchells. The rise of the Nazis and the resultant emigration of Jews and liberals from continental Europe brought pioneering foreign architects to London. One of the best-known buildings of the period, the De La Warr Pavilion at Bexhill-on-Sea, East Sussex (1935), was the result of a collaboration between Erich Mendelsohn, who had established his reputation in Germany, and the British-educated Russian Serge Chermayeff. The curved form of its glazed stair-tower and the fully glazed facade to the sea were made possible by using a steel frame to carry the structural loads – the wall was just a skin to keep out the wind and rain. This same partnership designed a house at 64 Old Church Street, Chelsea (1935–6), immediately next door to one by the exiled founder of the German Bauhaus design school, Walter Gropius, and his new British architectural partner Maxwell Fry.

One Modern Movement structure which really caught the public imagination was the Penguin Pool (1934) at London Zoo, the work of Tecton, a firm founded by Russian émigré Berthold Lubetkin and a group of young British architecture graduates. This bold piece of sculpture made use of reinforced concrete technology to intertwine two spiral ramps. Although it is visually stunning, its designers thought of it in very functional terms – they explained that the ramps were graded and stepped in order that the penguins should perform in an entertaining way for visitors.

Below: The Penguin Pool at London Zoo

BERKSHIRE, BUCKINGHAMSHIRE & OXFORDSHIRE

Local geology has had a distinctive influence over thousands of years on the pattern of settlement in these three counties. Different types of rock run in bands from the north-east to the south-west: the limestones of the Cotswolds; the clay vales of Oxford and Aylesbury; the chalk of the Chilterns and the Berkshire Downs. Through all three counties runs the River Thames, in the valley of which have been found the earliest remains of human activity from the time of the ice ages.

The whole of the Upper Thames Valley was settled in prehistoric times, as testified by the barrows where Neolithic and early Bronze Age people buried their dead, such as the group at Lambourn Seven Barrows in Berkshire, and the Iron Age hill-forts, such as Uffington Castle. Further evidence of early settlement is provided in a complex of crop-marks, with perhaps the

most significant group around Dorchester in Oxfordshire. The town was important in Roman times, and remained so when St Birinus converted the Anglo-Saxons here in the 630s.

By the time of the Norman Conquest Oxford was an important town and the

The entrance to Wayland's Smithy, a prehistoric long barrow in Oxfordshire

Normans established a castle there, the motte, or mound, of which survives. Oxford acquired its earliest college buildings in the 13th century, and began a path of development as a centre of learning and of outstanding architecture which has continued ever since.

Much of the prosperity of the later Middle Ages – sufficient to fund the building of houses such as Minster Lovell or churches like that at Rycote – was based on wool. After the Reformation grand houses were constructed for the aristocracy, such as Blenheim Palace in the 18th century. The arrival of the railways led to the rapid growth of settlements on the outskirts of London, and the process continued in the second half of the 20th century with the creation of new towns such as Milton Keynes.

DONNINGTON CASTLE

Donnington Castle is reached by a short walk up a grassy hill. It stands overlooking the Lambourn Valley in an important strategic position commanding the crossing of major north–south and east–west routes.

History

The manor of Donnington was held by the Abberbury family from 1287, and in 1386 Sir Richard Abberbury was granted a licence 'to crenellate

The imposing gatehouse of Donnington Castle

and fortify a castle at Donyngton, Berks' by Richard II. Sir Richard had been a companion of Richard II's father, Edward the Black Prince, at the battles of Crécy and Poitiers.

The castle consisted originally of a curtain wall with four round corner towers, two square wall towers and a substantial gatehouse, constructed around a courtyard in the style typical of the fortified residences of the period. Accommodation was provided in the towers or in buildings within the courtyard, set against the castle walls. The courtyard buildings are likely to have been of timber construction and possibly included a hall, a kitchen and lodgings for guests.

In the early 15th century the castle was held by Thomas Chaucer, son of the poet Geoffrey Chaucer, and later passed into the ownership of the Crown. Henry VIII is reported to have stayed here in 1539 and Elizabeth I in 1568.

During the Civil War Charles I set up his headquarters in Oxford and in 1643 dispatched Sir John Boys, with 200 foot soldiers, 25 cavalry and sufficient cannon to resist a siege, to take possession of Donnington from the Parliamentarian John Packer. Having taken the castle, Boys built defences around the lower slopes of the hill in the shape of a star, the projections providing sites for gun emplacements that gave a good field of fire. Between 1644 and 1646 the castle was attacked many times, twice being relieved by the king in person. Only when the Royalist cause appeared hopeless did Boys surrender to the Parliamentarian troops, after first obtaining the king's permission to do so.

Parliament voted to demolish the badly damaged castle in 1646 and only the gatehouse was left standing. This was restored to John Packer. The building passed to the guardianship of the state in 1946.

Description

The gatehouse, which is two storeys high and is roofed at battlement level, survives well. It serves as evidence for the luxury and privacy enjoyed by

Sir Richard Abberbury, whose private quarters would have been situated within this part of the castle. The gate passage has a finely vaulted ceiling, while elegant stone string courses with carved gargoyles decorate the outside. At the rear of the gatehouse the fireplaces and doors indicate the floor levels. Patches of brickwork show where the gatehouse was damaged during the Civil War sieges.

The external walls of the castle have been rebuilt to a height of 0.5m (2ft) and indicate its original layout. The Civil War defences survive as a series of scarps and platforms around the slopes of the hill.

The rear of the castle's gatehouse, with fireplaces and doorways indicating floor levels

I mile N
of Newbury
off B4494
OS Map 174,
ref SU 461692
Exterior viewing
only

95

ABINGDON COUNTY HALL

Abingdon County Hall has dominated the Market Place, in the heart of Abingdon, since the late 17th century. The town of Abingdon, initially formed as a settlement around its powerful abbey (founded in AD 675), developed into a prosperous market town owing to its flourishing wool trade. Formerly in Berkshire, Abingdon vied with Reading as the county town, and the County Hall

Abingdon County Hall, seen from East St Helen Street

stands today as testimony to the town's bid for this honour.

Constructed between 1678 and 1682, the old town hall has the typical combination for the period of a market space sheltering under a courtroom. Examples of this type of building that are earlier in date survive elsewhere as timber-framed free-standing town halls. Abingdon gains architectural distinction, however, from being built in Oxfordshire limestone; it is a monumental presence despite its compact site.

At the time that the County Hall was built, architecture in England was rapidly absorbing a number of different design influences from the Netherlands, France, Germany and Italy. These can be grouped under the umbrella term of baroque architecture. Architects working in England in the later 17th century produced individual responses to adapt elements of this European style to the existing English taste for Dutch-influenced, rather delicate, architectural form and detailing.

Sir Christopher Wren is the most celebrated architect of this period working in this idiom, and in the 1670s he was busy on the designs for rebuilding St Paul's Cathedral. It has been suggested that Abingdon County Hall was one of his designs, and it was certainly constructed by two men he respected and worked with closely: Christopher Kempster, master mason, and John Scarborough, clerk of works.

The monumental character of the building is derived from the giant Corinthian pilasters that rise from ground level through both storeys. They appear to support the weighty structure of the roof, and evoke the forms of temple architecture. The baroque aspect of the design comes from the giant form of the pilasters and the absence of a visible basement to act as a platform for them.

The arched windows, which echo the arched arcade below, are a typical baroque window shape. Otherwise, at roof level, the dormer windows, balustrade and cupola could easily be found on grand country and town houses of the 1660s and 1670s much less influenced by the baroque.

English baroque buildings are well represented in this region. Nearby Oxford has fine examples of the later decades of English baroque, seen in the university's colleges, libraries and chapels. North-west of Oxford,

The giant Corinthian pilasters on the exterior of Abingdon County Hall, built 1678–82 in the baroque style

Blenheim Palace is an extraordinary example of a Baroque country house. It has all the baroque characteristics: monumental form, massive blocks of building advancing and receding and dramatic detailing.

As an early 18th-century writer once observed, Abingdon County Hall is certainly 'a Market house of most curious Ashler workmanship which may challenge the Preeminence of any in England.'

In Abingdon, 7 miles S of Oxford, in Market Place *OS Map 164, ref SU 498971* Open 10.30 am– 4.30 pm daily Closed 25–26 Dec and during exhibition changeovers Tel: 01235 523703

Bishop Odo of Bayeux, depicted in the late 11th-century Bayeux Tapestry

The earthworks forming Deddington Castle lie in a rural location to the south-east of the village of Deddington. No stonework is visible above ground today, but the site is nevertheless a striking one owing to the scale of the earthworks – the rampart is 15m (49ft) high in places – and the size of the enclosed area.

At the time of the Domesday survey in 1087 the site was held by Odo, Bishop of Bayeux (who is thought to have commissioned the famous tapestry). The half-brother of William the Conqueror, Odo held substantial power in England after the Norman Conquest of 1066, where he was ruthless in his suppression of native rebellion. As Odo's Oxfordshire base, Deddington would have played a significant role in the Norman domination of the region.

Archaeological excavations have revealed that the site was already

Deddington Castle's high rampart walls enclosed a large bailey

View of the enclosure, looking south-west

occupied before the castle was built there. Fragmentary buildings and artefacts from the late Saxon period have been found in the western bailey and beneath the castle ramparts.

The entrance to the site opens onto an enclosure approximately 200m (219 yds) wide. This large, flat area was enclosed in the late 11th century by a bank and a ditch, to create a bailey. A motte (or mound) was built up on the eastern edge of this enclosure. Excavations have revealed that an earlier timber building was replaced in about 1160 by a stone-built structure to the west of the mound. An inner bailey was then constructed around this building, and by the end of the 12th century the motte had been levelled and a curtain wall erected, with stone towers and a gatehouse that led to the outer bailey. The remains of a 13th-century chapel have been discovered, with those of a slightly earlier one buried beneath them. From the end of the 13th century the castle fell into disrepair, and became a quarry for local building stone.

A second enclosure to the east of the site contained a complex of four fish ponds.

S of B4031 on E side of Deddington, 17 miles N of Oxford on A423 OS Map 151, ref SP 472316

99

The ruins of Minster Lovell Hall are located in a beautiful rural setting beside the River Windrush. The hall is approached from the north, through the adjacent churchyard, but there is a footpath along the Windrush valley from the east, which would originally have provided access to the site.

History

There has been a manor house at Minster Lovell since at least the 12th century, but the major part of the ruins seen today are those of a large new house built by William, Baron of Lovell and Holand, in the 1430s after his return from the French wars. Through marriage and good fortune William was one of the richest men in England, and he built his house as a demonstration of his wealth.

William's son John, a prominent Lancastrian and servant of Henry VI, was rewarded with the position of master forester of the neighbouring royal forest, Wychwood. By contrast, John's son Francis, the ninth baron, served the Yorkist cause, and was created Viscount Lovell by Richard III.

Following the defeat of the House of York in the battle of Bosworth in 1485 the hall passed into the hands of the Crown and eventually, in 1602, into the possession of the successful lawyer Sir Edward Coke. His descendant Thomas Coke, later Earl of Leicester, was in residence in 1721 and in 1728 he assumed the title Lord Lovell of Minster Lovell. The hall was, however, abandoned in

Minster Lovell Hall from the south-west

favour of the Cokes' seat at Holkham, Norfolk, begun in the 1730s, and in about 1747 most of the buildings were dismantled, the east and west ranges and the kitchens being demolished for building stone.

Description

The buildings are grouped around a central courtyard in a form characteristic of a late medieval manor house. In the 15th century the household was the central institution in the life of the aristocracy. Good lordship and hospitality were fundamental to the maintenance of the loyalties – both in peacetime and during local or national conflicts – on which late medieval society relied.

The porch to the north wing, approached down a patterned, cobbled pathway, has a striking vaulted ceiling. Beyond the porch is the great hall, the walls of which still stand to a height, in places, of 12m (39ft). West of the hall, and separated

Reconstruction drawing of Minster Lovell Hall as it might have appeared in the 18th century

from it by the width of the room that would formerly have been used as a parlour with a chamber above, lies the north-west building. The east and west walls of this structure still stand. In the 19th century an attempt to convert it into a barn with two opposing doors led to the collapse of the roof; a small fireplace let into the north wall is evidence of a cottage constructed subsequently within the walls. To the north of the hall, ground-floor apartments lay beneath the private chapel on the first floor, their windows looking out on to the outer court. A blocked-up gateway indicates the former access from this court to the church.

The east wing of the manor house comprised the stable, kitchen and other service buildings, and the outline of these structures can still be seen on the ground. The hearth to the big range fire is still visible in the thick south wall of the kitchen, while close to the west wall is the old well. Also surviving is the stone floor of the stable. The wide passage between the stable and the kitchen formed the principal entrance to the courtyard and house.

In the west wing foundations reveal the presence of five ground-floor rooms. Stone water tanks and channels suggest that these buildings were later adapted for use as a small tannery, and there is a reference to a 'tannehouse' in a document of 1536.

The four-storey tower at the south-west corner is thought to date to the later 15th century, the period of Francis Lovell's ownership. Access to the first floor was by external stairs, the two upper floors being reached by the octagonal turret in the angle between the tower and the west wing.

To the west and south-east of the ruins two large fish ponds, which supplied the household with fresh fish, survive. The manor's 15th-century dovecote, a small circular building with a conical roof, survives intact to the north-east of the site.

Above: The interior of Minster Lovell's dovecote (detail)

Facing page: The south-west tower, with the hall beyond

Adjacent to Minster Lovell church, 3 miles W of Witney, off A40
OS Map 164, ref SP 325113

North Hinksey Conduit House, standing on a hillside above the city of Oxford

North Hinksey Conduit House is located on a hillside with views over the busy Oxford ring road to the spires of the city below.

History

The conduit house, which covers and protects a shallow well, was built in about 1617 as part of a system constructed to take clean drinking water from the springs at North Hinksey downhill to the Carfax Conduit, a fountain in the centre of Oxford. The lawyer Otho Nicholson promoted the system, and erected the

ornate fountain to mark James I's visit to Oxford. The fountain was dismantled as part of street improvements in 1787, but re-erected in the same year by the second Lord Harcourt as an eye-catcher at Nuneham Park, a few miles outside the city (this is not open to the public).

The ditch through which water flowed downhill from North Hinksey is no longer visible at ground level and has been cut and removed at many points. The conduit house itself, however, survives in its original location as a fine example of early civic clean-water provision.

The Carfax Conduit at Nuneham Park, photographed by Henry Taunt, 1882

Description

The conduit house is a single-storey structure, built of dressed limestone. Recent repair work has involved the replacement of some of the stones with a finer-grained limestone. The stone roof and some of the coping stones are modern.

The building measures 13m (43ft) by 8m (26ft), the walls standing to a height of about 4m (13ft) at the gable ends. The side walls each have two gabled buttresses. A round-headed doorway provides an entrance to the structure on the front gable end, above which is carved the coat of arms of Otho Nicholson. Narrow, two-light vents pierce the structure on both gable ends. There is some beautifully chiselled graffiti from the late 17th and 18th centuries on the exterior of the building.

The centre of Oxford in the 18th century, with the Carfax Conduit on the left

Located off a track leading from Harcourt Hill. There is no parking in the immediate vicinity. Approach on foot from Botley or North Hinksey, or use the footpath from Ferry Hinksey Lane (starts near to the railway station). In North Hinksey off A34, 2¹/₂ mile W of Oxford.
OS Map 164, ref SP 495050
Exterior viewing only 10am–4pm

The remains of the Roman villa are located in a peaceful rural landscape, within a loop of the River Evenlode, which flows gently past the site to the north and west.

As visitors approach along a bridleway the site is visible below to the right, and its rectangular arrangement is immediately apparent. This was a 'courtyard villa', having a range of buildings on each of three sides of a rectangle, with a corridor and gatehouse closing the courtyard on the fourth side.

Significant finds of pre-Roman Iron Age pottery and other features beneath the former south-west range show evidence of earlier occupation, and it is known that the development of the site was lengthy and complex.

The Iron Age settlement was superseded by the first Roman development in the 1st or early 2nd century AD. This phase consisted of three buildings along the line of what was to become the north-west range, one of which was a bath-house. Another structure served as a linking corridor. Early in the 3rd century were added the south-west and north-east wings, partially enclosing the courtyard. These wings were later extended and the original north-west

The ruins of the Roman villa at North Leigh

range entirely rebuilt, probably in the early 4th century. At this stage the villa incorporated 4 bath suites, 16 mosaic floors and 11 rooms with under-floor heating. Aerial photographs have revealed that there were further buildings beyond the south-west range – perhaps including an aisled barn or hall – which may have formed a home farm for the villa. The villa was abandoned when the Romans withdrew from Britain in the 5th century.

North Leigh ranks among the larger villas of Roman Britain. A few of these villas may have been the residences of Roman officials, but the majority are now thought to have been the homes of leading members of the native population who were co-opted into the empire and rewarded with lavish buildings and a superior way of life.

North Leigh Roman Villa is noted for the 3rd-century mosaic floor displayed on the site. (This floor was lifted and relaid in 1929.) The shed over the mosaic floor is one of two

A large fragment of the mosaic floors, displayed on site

built by the owner of the site, the Duke of Marlborough, following excavations between 1812 and 1814 and after two other mosaics had been destroyed by souvenir hunters.

It is not known when the small cottage, formerly used by a custodian, was erected; it was first recorded in 1921, and may date from the 1812–14 excavation work.

Access is on foot for 550m (600yds) along a bridleway. The mosaic tile floor is enclosed behind a viewing window. 2 miles N of North Leigh, 10 miles W of Oxford, off A4095
OS Map 164, ref SP 397154

The chalk downland of south-east England is a landscape modified over thousands of years by the lives and work of men and women. Today it is a rolling expanse of hills and dry valleys, either ploughed or covered in springy turf with unique flora and fauna. Patches of grassland unploughed since the Roman period attract rare plants such as the burnt orchid and butterflies, including the chalkhill blue and Adonis blue.

The earliest colonisers of the British Isles hunted and scavenged over the Downs, as evidence at the internationally significant site of Boxgrove, West Sussex, shows. Here, unique fragments of anatomically pre-modern humans from about 400,000 BC have been found, together with their stone tools and the animals they hunted. They lived in a temperate period between glaciations, when the Downs were covered in primeval forest and the Boxgrove quarries formed a subtropical lagoon. Once the climate warmed up, new woodland populated by deer, elk and pig, providing food for Middle Stone Age hunters, covered the Downs.

Gradual tree clearance occurred from 4300 BC, creating small, short-lived fields for semi-nomadic groups of Late Stone Age farmers. As well as exploiting the easily worked, light soils, the farmers extracted flint from quarries as the raw material for tools such as axes, knives, scrapers and arrowheads. These artefacts are still found widely scattered over the Downs.

The first farmers left permanent monuments in the landscape in the form of long barrows and causewayed enclosures. In about 2500 BC a new type of monument began to be constructed, with a greater emphasis on the individual rather than the collective ancestors venerated earlier. This was the earthen round barrow, or burial mound, many hundreds of which still stand

Left: Flint mines and hill-fort at Cissbury Ring, West Sussex

surviving contemporary hill-forts are the most dramatic reminder of these peoples. Some of these enclosures, like Danebury in Hampshire, were fortified settlements; others, like Caburn in East Sussex, were more likely ritual centres.

During the Roman period the Downs were used intensivelyfor agriculture. Medieval exploitation of the landscape set the more familiar pattern of grazing sheep. Despite this succession of activity over millennia, the Downs today still record the lives of the first farmers and their impact on the land.

Above left: Neolithic flint mines at Angmering, West Sussex

Below: Ancient burial sites, visible as crop-marks at Eynsham, Oxfordshire

across the downland of southern Britain. This period also saw the arrival of bronze tools. During the Bronze Age the first permanent farmsteads and fields were established. This was made possible by the introduction of manuring and crop rotation in about 1000 BC, evidence of which was discovered at the Bronze Age village of Black Patch, East Sussex. Rectangular fields from this date survive as lynchets, or field banks, on the Downs.

This system of rectangular fields was massively expanded in the pre-Roman Iron Age, the period of 600 years or so before the Roman administration of Britain. There are many Iron Age villages and farmsteads like that reconstructed on Butser Hill in Hampshire on the Downs, but the

These three prehistoric sites are located beside the Ridgeway, the ancient route that stretched from Dorset to the Wash and that still traverses the chalk ridges of the Berkshire Downs.

Uffington Castle

The Iron Age hill-fort known as Uffington Castle occupies the summit of Whitehorse Hill. It consists of a large enclosure, measuring about 220m by 160m (721ft by 525ft), surrounded by a wide chalk-stone bank or inner rampart, about 12m (39ft) in width and 2.5m (8ft) in height, and formerly lined with sarsen (sandstone) stones. Around this is a grass-covered ditch about 3m (10ft) deep and a further, smaller bank forming an outer rampart. A causeway, flanked by the out-turned ends of the inner rampart, provides an entrance to the site from the west. This would have been closed by a gate.

Postholes and pits revealed during archaeological excavations serve as evidence of structures built within the enclosure during the hill-fort's occupation, while pottery and coins have been found in burial chambers close by. The Iron Age buildings are likely to have been large round huts, each housing an extended family group. In the Middle Ages the land within the enclosure was ploughed and earthworks mark the ridge and furrow pattern of cultivation.

Large Iron Age hill-forts are rare. Most are located on the high chalklands of the southern counties of England, and Uffington Castle is regarded as an outstanding example.

The western ramparts of Uffington Castle on Whitehorse Hill

The White Horse

Situated 170m (558ft) to the north-east of the hill-fort – and visible from a distance of several miles – is the striking chalk-cut figure of a horse. The White Horse, which measures

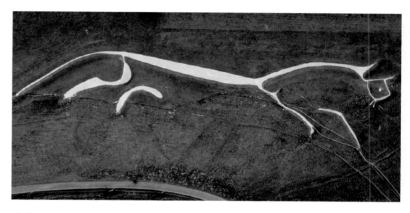

111m (364ft) in length from the tip of its tail to its ear, is generally thought to date, with the hill-fort, from the Iron Age. It may have been a territorial marker or a fertility symbol – its function is not certain. Once every seven years from at least 1677 until the late 18th century a midsummer 'scouring festival' was held, during which local people cleaned the chalk outline of the horse and enjoyed a celebratory feast within the hill-fort. The shape of the horse has changed over the centuries. The present outline may be only a part of

the original: aerial photography shows that a larger, more conventional shape of a horse lies beneath. The loss of shape has been caused by slippage of the top soil and by repeated recutting. The head currently has a prominent 'eye', and tusk-like 'beak' at its mouth.

Dragon Hill

Local legend associates the horse with St George and the Dragon, hence the name of nearby Dragon Hill. This is a round mound, about 10m (33ft) high with a flattened top, likely to have been formed by glacial erosion.

The huge figure of the White Horse, cut into the chalk hillside along the Ridgeway

S of B4507,
7 miles W
of Wantage
OS Map 174,
ref SU 301866

111

Above: The interior of the burial chamber of Wayland's Smithy

Right: Sarsen stones marking the entrance to the burial mound

This prehistoric long barrow, or burial chamber, lies on the right of the path from Whitehorse Hill along the Ridgeway in a south-westerly direction. This was the ancient hilltop track that stretched from Dorset to the Wash and still survives in the chalk ridges of the Berkshire Downs.

Long barrows, constructed as earthen or dry-stone mounds with flanking ditches, belong to the early Neolithic period, from about 4000 to 3000 BC. These barrows served as burial places for early farming communities and are among the oldest visible monuments surviving in the landscape today.

The mound at Wayland's Smithy, dating from the period 3700 to 3400 BC, is constructed of chalkstone and turf and measures about 55m by 14m (180ft by 46ft). It is edged with small sarsen (sandstone) stones, each of which is about 0.3m (1ft) in height. A dry-stone wall forms a facade at the southern end of the barrow, against which are set four large sarsen stones, standing to a height above ground of 3m (10ft). Between these stones is located the entrance to a narrow,

stone-lined passage just less than 2m (7ft) high, which led into the mound to a distance of about 6m (20ft). The passage has two small side chambers, forming a cross-shaped plan. The partial skeletons of at least eight people were found within the mound when the site was excavated in 1919–20, although there is evidence that the site was disturbed in Roman times and further remains may have been lost.

During excavation in the 1960s a smaller and earlier mound was found lying beneath the barrow, half its height, having been incorporated into the later structure. Consisting of stone slabs and timber posts and roofed with chalkstone, the mound covered a stone platform on which the partial skeletons of at least 14 people have been found, most of them young and one a child of nine years. This mound, too, was surrounded by sarsen stones. Just under 1m (3ft) in height, these were placed against the sides of the mound rather than being set into the ground.

Flanking the mound, though no longer visible at ground level, are two ditches from which the material to build the mound was excavated. Infilled in the ancient past, these survive as buried features. Finds of Bronze Age metalwork and Iron Age and Roman pottery indicate later activity in the area of the barrow. Field ditches and terraces, probably of Iron Age or Roman date, are part of a more extensive field system, which may have used the barrow as a marker.

Wayland the Smith was a figure from Saxon legend who was believed to inhabit the mound; if a horse were to be left there alone with a silver coin the traveller would return to find the horse shod and the coin gone.

Above: Other sarsen stones flanking the sides of the prehistoric long barrow at Wayland's Smithy

On the Ridgeway (access on foot) ³/₄ mile NE of B4000, Ashbury to Lambourn road
OS Map 178, ref TQ 759706

Thirty-seven English Heritage sites in London and the South East are staffed. Most have a separate guidebook, which can be bought at the site's gift shop or through mail order. These sites charge an admission fee, although admission is free to members of English Heritage (see inside back cover). Please note that sites listed here as opening 1 April will open for Easter if it is earlier. Full details of admission charges, access and opening times for all English Heritage sites are given in the *English Heritage Members' and Visitors' Handbook* and on our website (www.english-heritage.org.uk). Full details of English Heritage's publications can be found in the *Publishing Catalogue*. To obtain a free copy of the catalogue, and to order English Heritage publications, please contact:

English Heritage Postal Sales
c/o Gillards, Trident Works,
Temple Cloud, Bristol BS39 5AZ

Tel: 01761 452966 Fax: 01761 453408
E-mail: ehsales@gillards.com

APSLEY HOUSE
HYDE PARK CORNER

Designed in the 1770s, Apsley House became the home of the Duke of Wellington in 1817, and was later enlarged by the architect Benjamin Dean Wyatt in 1819 and 1828–9.

Please call for admission prices and opening dates and times: 020 7499 5676.

149 Piccadilly.
OS Map 176, ref TQ 284799.

CHAPTER HOUSE AND PYX CHAMBER
WESTMINSTER ABBEY.

Built in about 1250, the Chapter House was originally used by Benedictine monks for their daily meetings. It later became the meeting place of the King's Great Council and the Commons, predecessors of today's Parliament. The 11th-century Pyx Chamber was used as a monastic and royal treasury.

Please call for admission prices and opening dates and times: 020 7654 4834. The Chapter House is managed by the Dean and Chapter of Westminster.

Access through the cloister from Dean's Yard.
OS Map 177, ref TQ 299795.

CHISWICK HOUSE
CHISWICK

Chiswick House was designed and built in the 18th century by the third Earl of Burlington, who aimed to create the kind of classical house and

garden found in the suburbs of ancient Rome. The interiors were designed by William Kent.

Please call for admission prices and opening dates and times: 020 8995 0508.

Burlington Lane, W4.
OS Map 176, refTQ 210775.

ELTHAM PALACE
ELTHAM

When textile magnates Stephen and Virginia Courtauld built this Art Deco mansion beside the great hall of medieval Eltham Palace, they created a showpiece of 1930s design.

Please call for admission prices and opening dates and times: 020 8294 2548.

Junction 3 on the M25, then A20 to Eltham; off Court Rd SE9.
OS Map 177, refTQ 424740.

JEWEL TOWER
WESTMINSTER

The Jewel Tower, or 'King's Privy Wardrobe', was built in about 1365 to house the treasures of Edward III.

Please call for admission prices and opening dates and times: 020 7222 2219.

Abingdon Street, opposite the southern end of the Houses of Parliament.
OS Map 177, refTQ 301793.

MARBLE HILL HOUSE
TWICKENHAM

This Palladian villa is the last complete surviving example of the elegant villas which once bordered the River Thames between Richmond and Hampton Court in the 18th century.

Please call for admission prices and opening dates and times: 020 8892 5115.

Richmond Rd, Twickenham.
OS Map 176, refTQ 173736.

RANGER'S HOUSE – THE WERNHER COLLECTION
GREENWICH PARK

The elegant Georgian villa of Ranger's House, on the edge of Greenwich Park, is home to the Wernher Collection, a stunning display of medieval and Renaissance works of art.

Please call for admission prices and opening dates and times: 020 8853 0035.

Chesterfield Walk, Blackheath SE10.
OS Map 177, ref TQ 388769.

WELLINGTON ARCH
HYDE PARK CORNER

Originally known as Green Park Arch, this monument was adorned with a statue of the first Duke of Wellington from 1846 to 1883. It was completed in 1830 by the architect Decimus Burton and moved to its present site in 1882–3. The spectacular bronze sculpture depicts the angel of peace descending on the chariot of war.

Please call for admission prices and opening dates and times: 020 7930 2726.

Hyde Park Corner.
OS Map 176, ref TQ 284798.

APPULDURCOMBE HOUSE
ISLE OF WIGHT

The shell of Appuldurcombe, once the grandest house on the Isle of Wight, stands in grounds designed by 'Capability' Brown.

Please call for admission prices and opening dates and times: 01983 852484. Managed by Mr and Mrs Owen.

¹/2 mile from Wroxall, off B3327.
OS Map 196, ref SZ 543800.

1066 BATTLE OF HASTINGS, ABBEY AND BATTLEFIELD
EAST SUSSEX

King William founded Battle Abbey to atone for the loss of life during the Conquest.

Please call for admission prices and opening dates and times: 01424 773792.

In Battle, at S end of High St. For Battle turn off A21 on to A2100.
OS Map 199, ref TQ 749157.

BAYHAM OLD ABBEY
KENT

These ruins of a house of 'White Canons' date from about 1208. They are set in a landscape that

was shaped in the 18th century. Rooms in the Georgian Dower House are open to the public.

Please call for admission prices and opening dates and times: 01892 890381.

1³/₄ miles W of Lamberhurst, off B2169.
OS Map 188, ref TQ 650365.

BISHOP'S WALTHAM PALACE
HAMPSHIRE

These are the ruins of a medieval palace used by the bishops of Winchester as they travelled round their diocese. Much of what can be seen today is the work of William Wykeham, who was bishop from 1367.

Please call for admission prices and opening dates and times: 01489 892460.

In Bishop's Waltham.
OS Map 185, ref SU 552174.

CALSHOT CASTLE
HAMPSHIRE

This artillery fort, built by Henry VIII to defend the entrance to Southampton Water, later became a sea-plane base.

Please call for admission prices and opening dates and times: 02380 892023 or when castle is closed 02380 892077. Managed by Hampshire County Council.

On spit, 2 miles SE of Fawley, off B3053.
OS Map 196, ref SU 489025.

CAMBER CASTLE
EAST SUSSEX

One of a chain of fortresses built by Henry VIII to defend the coast from invasion.

There are monthly guided walks round Rye Harbour Nature Reserve, including the castle.

Please call for admission prices and opening dates and times: 01797 223862. Managed by Rye Harbour Nature Reserve.

1 mile walk across fields, off A259; 1 mile S of Rye, off Harbour Road.
No vehicle access.
OS Map 189, ref TQ 922185.

CARISBROOKE CASTLE
ISLE OF WIGHT

The castle was built in 1100 in this dominant hilltop position, on the site of an earlier timber fort. In 1293 it passed to the Crown and became enormously significant in the defence of the Isle of Wight. It also served as a prison, and in 1647 Charles I was imprisoned here.

Please call for admission prices and opening dates and times: 01983 522107.

1¼ miles SW of Newport.
OS Map 196, ref SZ 486878.

DEAL CASTLE
KENT

Deal Castle is among the earliest and most elaborate of the chain of coastal fortresses erected at great speed between 1539 and 1540 by order of Henry VIII, who feared an invasion by the Catholic powers of Europe.

Please call for admission prices and opening dates and times: 01304 372762.

SW of Deal town centre.
OS Map 179, ref TR 378522.

DOVER CASTLE AND THE SECRET WARTIME TUNNELS
KENT

Dover Castle was pivotal to the defence of England's shores from its Norman beginnings, through Hubert de Burgh's resistance against Prince Louis of France in the 13th century and Henry VIII's defences against Catholic invasion three centuries later, to the evacuation of 338,000 troops from the beaches of Dunkirk, France, in May 1940.

Entry includes admission to tours of the Secret Wartime Tunnels. Please call for admission prices and opening dates and times: 01304 211067.

E of Dover town centre.
OS Map 179, ref TR 325419.

DOWN HOUSE
KENT

Down House was the home of Charles Darwin, and it was here that he wrote *On the Origin of Species by Means of Natural Selection*, the book that both scandalised and revolutionised the Victorian world when it was published in 1859.

Please call for admission prices and opening dates and times: 01689 859119.

Luxted Rd, Downe; off A21 or A233.
OS Map 177, ref TQ 431611.

DYMCHURCH MARTELLO TOWER
KENT

The best-preserved of a chain of ingeniously designed artillery towers, built at vulnerable points around the south-east coast to resist

invasion by Napoleon.

Open August Bank Holiday and Heritage Open Days. Please call for admission prices and opening dates and times: 01304 211067.

In Dymchurch, access from High St only.
*OS Map 189,
ref TR 102292.*

FARNHAM CASTLE KEEP
SURREY

This motte-and-bailey castle has been continuously occupied since the 12th century and was once one of the seats of the Bishop of Winchester.

Please call for admission prices and opening dates and times: 01252 713393.

½ mile N of Farnham town centre, on A287.
*OS Map 186,
ref SU 837473.*

FORT BROCKHURST
HAMPSHIRE

One of a number of forts built in the 1850s to protect Portsmouth and its vital dockyard. Largely unaltered, the parade ground, gun ramps and moated keep can all be viewed.

The fort opens occasionally for pre-booked tours and Heritage Open Days. Please call for details: 01424 775705.

Off A32, in Gunner's Way, Elson; on N side of Gosport.
OS Map 196, ref SU 596021.

FORT CUMBERLAND
HAMPSHIRE

Constructed between 1785 and 1810 in a pentagonal shape by the Duke of Cumberland, this is one of England's most impressive pieces of 18th-century defensive architecture.

The fort opens occasionally for pre-booked tours and Heritage Open Days. Please call for details: 01424 775705.

In Portsmouth's Eastney district on the estuary approach, via Henderson Rd off Eastney Rd, or from the Esplanade.
OS Map 196, ref SZ 683993.

HURST CASTLE
HAMPSHIRE

One of the most sophisticated fortresses built by Henry VIII, and later strengthened in the 19th and 20th centuries, the castle commands the Needles Passage to the Solent.

Please call for admission prices and opening dates and times: 01590 642344. Managed by Hurst Castle Services.

On Pebble Spit S of Keyhaven; best approached by ferry from Keyhaven – call 01590 642500 for ferry details.
OS Map 196, ref SZ 318897.

LULLINGSTONE ROMAN VILLA
KENT

The villa was built in about AD 100 but extended during 300 years of Roman occupation. Much is still visible today, including the mosaic-tiled floors and wall paintings and the remains of the extensive 4th-century bath complex.

Please call for admission prices and opening dates and times: 01322 863467.

1/2 mile SW of Eynsford.
OS Map 177, ref TQ 530651.

MAISON DIEU
KENT

This medieval building, forming part of a hospital, royal lodging and almshouse, houses Roman artefacts from nearby sites.

Please call for admission prices and opening dates and times: 01795 534542. Managed by The Faversham Society.

In Ospringe on A2; 1/2 mile W of Faversham.
OS Map 179, ref TR 313407.

MEDIEVAL MERCHANT'S HOUSE
HAMPSHIRE

John Fortin, a merchant who traded with Bordeaux, started building this house in Southampton in about 1290. It has been restored to its mid-14th-century appearance.

Please call for admission prices and opening dates and times: 02380 221503.

58 French St, 1/4 mile S of city centre, just off Castle Way (between High St and Bugle St).
OS Map 196, ref SU 419112.

MILTON CHANTRY
KENT

This small 14th-century building housed the chapel of a leper hospital and a family chantry. Dissolved during the Reformation, it later became a tavern and, in 1780, part of a fort.

Please call for admission prices and opening dates and times: 01474 321520. Managed by Gravesham Borough Council.

In New Tavern Fort Gardens; E of central Gravesend, off A226.
OS Map 177, ref TQ 653743.

OSBORNE HOUSE
ISLE OF WIGHT

Osborne House became the country residence of Queen Victoria in 1840, shortly after her marriage to Prince Albert. It comprises several wings, apartments and buildings, in a setting of terraces and parkland overlooking the Solent.

Open year-round but entry by guided tour only in winter. Please call for details and admission prices: 01983 200022.

1 mile SE of East Cowes.
OS Map 196, ref SZ 516948.

PEVENSEY CASTLE
EAST SUSSEX

This is one of Britain's oldest and most important strongholds, with fortifications surviving from three distinct periods: Roman, medieval and World War II.

Please call for admission prices and opening dates and times: 01323 762604.

In Pevensey off A259.
OS Map 199, ref TQ 645048.

MAJOR ENGLISH HERITAGE SITES

PORTCHESTER CASTLE

The most impressive and best-preserved of Roman Saxon Shore forts, Portchester is the only Roman stronghold in northern Europe whose multi-towered walls still mainly stand to their full original height. The huge fortress became a Norman castle in the 12th century, when a formidable tower keep was built in one corner.

Please call for admission prices and opening dates and times: 02392 378291.

On the S side of Portchester off A27; junction 11 on M27.
OS Map 196, ref SU 625046.

RICHBOROUGH ROMAN FORT

Now over two miles from the sea, this was probably the Romans' main entry port into Britain. Remains on the site date back to the invasion of AD 43.

Please call for admission prices and opening dates and times: 01304 612013.

At the A256/A257 roundabout take the road for Sandwich and then turn left at the fire station.
OS Map 179, ref TR 324602.

ROCHESTER CASTLE

Built on the Roman city wall, this Norman castle was a vital royal stronghold.

Please call for admission prices and opening dates and times: 01634 402276. Managed by Medway Council.

By Rochester Bridge on A2; junction 1 of M2 and junction 2 of M25.
OS Map 178, ref TQ 741686.

ROLLRIGHT STONES

These stones, comprising three groups known as the King's Men, the Whispering Knights and the King Stone, span nearly 2,000 years of the Neolithic and Bronze Ages.

All the stones are accessible sunrise to sunset, the Whispering Knights and the King Stone via a footpath. Entry to the King's Men is courtesy of the owner, who may levy a charge. Please call for details: 01553 631330. Managed by The Rollright Trust.

Off unclassified road between A44 and A3400; 3 miles NW of Chipping Norton, near villages of Little Rollright and Long Compton.
OS Map 151, ref SP 297309.

ST AUGUSTINE'S ABBEY
KENT

This great abbey, marking the rebirth of Christianity in southern England, was founded in AD 597 by St Augustine. Originally created as a burial place for the Anglo-Saxon kings of Kent, it is part of the Canterbury World Heritage Site.

Please call for admission prices and opening dates and times: 01227 767345.

In Canterbury, ¼ mile E of Cathedral Close.
OS Map 179, ref TR 155578.

UPNOR CASTLE
KENT

Upnor Castle was built in 1559 to protect the Royal Navy anchorage in the Medway. It saw action in 1667 when the Dutch navy sailed up the Medway to attack the dockyard at Chatham.

Please call for admission prices and opening dates and times: 01634 718742 or when castle is closed 01634 338110. Managed by Medway Council.

At Upnor, on unclassified road off A228.
OS Map 178, ref TQ 759706.

WALMER CASTLE AND GARDENS
KENT

Built as one of Henry VIII's coastal defences, in 1708 Walmer Castle became the official residence of the Lord Warden of the Cinque Ports and in this capacity was occupied by, among others, the Duke of Wellington and William Pitt the Younger. The late Queen Mother succeeded Sir Robert Menzies as Lord Warden, and the grounds contain the Queen Mother's Garden, designed by Penelope Hobhouse as a gift to her on her 95th birthday.

Please call for admission prices and opening dates and times: 01304 364288. Closed when the Lord Warden is in residence.

On coast S of Walmer, on A258; junction 13 of M20 or from M2 to Deal.
OS Map 179, ref TR 378501.

YARMOUTH CASTLE
ISLE OF WIGHT

This last addition to Henry VIII's coastal defences, which commands extensive views over the Solent, was completed in 1547.

Please call for admission prices and opening dates and times: 01983 760678.

In Yarmouth, adjacent to car ferry terminal.
OS Map 196, ref SZ 354898.

INDEX

INDEX

FURTHER READING

LONDON

Coombe Conduit

Forge, J L 'Coombe Hill Conduit Houses and the Water Supply of Hampton Court Palace', *Surrey Archaeological Collections* 56, 1959, pp. 3–14

Thurley, S *Hampton Court Palace*. New Haven and London: Yale University Press, 2003

London Wall

Milne, G *Roman London*. English Heritage Series. London: Batsford, 1995

Winchester Palace

Carlin, M 'The Reconstruction of Winchester House', *London Topographical Record* 25, 1985, pp. 35–57.

'Bankside' in *The Survey of London* Vol 22, pp. 45–56. London: City of Westminster, 1950

KENT, SURREY & SUSSEX

Boxgrove Priory

Fleming, L *The Chartulary of Boxgrove Priory*. Sussex Record Society 59. Lewes: Sussex Record Society, 1960

Ratcliff, R *The Story of Boxgrove Priory*. Chichester: Boxgrove Parochial Church Council, 1972

Bramber Castle

Erredge, H *The History of Bramber Castle*. Brighton, 1882

Eynsford Castle

Rigold, S E *Eynsford Castle, Kent*. London: RCHME, 1964

Faversham Stone Chapel

De la Bédoyère, G *Architecture in Roman Britain*. Princes Risborough: Shire, 2002

Fletcher, E and Meates, G W 'The Ruined Church of Stone-by-Faversham: second report', *Antiquaries Journal*, vol 57 (I), 1977, pp. 67–72

Kit's Coty House

Philp, B and Dutto, M, *The Medway Megaliths*. Kent Archaeological Trust, 1985

The Story of 'Kit's Coty House', Aylesford, Kent. London: R E Thomas, 1907

Old Soar Manor

Barnwell, P S and Adams, A T *The House Within – Interpreting Medieval Houses in Kent*. London: RCHME, 1994

Pearson, S *The Medieval Houses of Kent*: an Historical Analysis. London: RCHME, 1994

Wood, M *The English Medieval House*. London: Studio Editions, 1965

Wood, M *Old Soar*, Plaxtol, Kent. London: HMSO, 1950

Reculver Towers and Roman Fort
Richborough Roman Amphitheatre

Harris, S *Richborough and Reculver*. London: English Heritage, 2001

St Augustine's Cross

Gameson, R (ed) *St Augustine and the Conversion of England*. Stroud: Sutton, 1999

Hawkes, J *The Sandbach Crosses – Sign and Significance in Anglo-Saxon Sculpture*. London: Four Courts Press, 2002

Temple Manor

Rigold, S E *Temple Manor, Strood, Rochester, Kent*. London: English Heritage, 1990

Waverley Abbey

Ware, G *The White Monks of Waverley*. Farnham: Farnham and District Museum Society, 1976

Western Heights

Burridge, D *A Guide to the Western Heights Defences, Dover*. Dover: Kent Defence Research Group, 1993

Peverley, J *Dover's Hidden Fortress: The History and Preservation of the Western Heights Fortifications*. Dover: Dover Society, 1996

HAMPSHIRE & THE ISLE OF WIGHT

Flowerdown Barrows

Woodward, A *British Barrows: A Matter of Life and Death*. Stroud: Tempus, 2000

FURTHER READING

King James's and Landport Gates
Royal Garrison Church

Lilley, H T *Early Portsmouth Defences*. Portsmouth: Charpentier, 1923

Lloyd, D W *Buildings of Portsmouth and its Environs: A Survey of the Dockyard, Defences, Homes, Churches, Commercial, Civic and Public Buildings*. Portsmouth: City of Portsmouth, 1974

Netley Abbey

Hare, J 'Netley Abbey: Monastery, Mansion and Ruin', *Proceedings of the Hampshire Field Club* 49, 1993, pp. 207–27

Thompson, A H *Netley Abbey*, Hampshire. London: HMSO, 1973

Northington Grange

Liscombe, R W *William Wilkins, 1778–1839*. Cambridge: Cambridge University Press, 1980

Silchester Roman City Walls and Amphitheatre

De la Bédoyère, G *Roman Towns in Britain*. English Heritage Series. London: Batsford, 1992

Fulford, M G *Calleva Atrebatum: A guide to the Roman Town at Silchester*. Silchester: Calleva Museum, 1987

Fulford, M G *The Silchester Amphitheatre: Excavations of 1979–85*. Britannia Monograph Series 10. London: Society for the Promotion of Roman Studies, 1989

Titchfield Abbey

Graham, R *Titchfield Abbey, Hampshire*. London: RCHME, 1985

Wolvesey Castle

Biddle, M *Wolvesey – The Old Bishop's Palace*, Winchester, Hampshire. London: English Heritage, 1986

James, T B *Winchester*. English Heritage Series. London: Batsford, 1997

Riall, N *Henry of Blois, Bishop of Winchester*. Hampshire Papers 5. Winchester: Hampshire County Council, 1994

Wareham, J *Three Palaces of the Bishops of Winchester*. London: English Heritage, 2000

St Catherine's Oratory

Hockey, S F *Insula Vecta: The Isle of Wight in the Middle Ages*. Chichester: Phillimore, 1982

BERKSHIRE, BUCKINGHAMSHIRE & OXFORDSHIRE

Abingdon County Hall

Gilyard-Beer, R *The Abingdon County Hall*. London: Department of the Environment, 1981

Morrice, R *The Buildings of Britain: A Guide and Gazetteer: Stuart and Baroque*. London: Barrie and Jenkins, 1982

Deddington Castle

Ivens, R J *Deddington Castle, Oxfordshire: A Summary of Excavations 1977–1979*. Council for British Archaeology Group 9. Council for British Archaeology, 1983

Ivens, R J 'Deddington Castle, Oxfordshire, and the English honour of Odo of Bayeux', *Oxoniensia* 49, 1984, pp. 101–19

Donnington Castle

Wood, M *Donnington Castle, Berkshire*. London: HMSO, 1964

Minster Lovell Hall and Dovecote

Hansell, P *Dovecotes*. Princes Risborough: Shire, 2001

Taylor, A J *Minster Lovell Hall, Oxfordshire*. London: English Heritage, 1990

North Hinksey Conduit House

Cole, J C 'Carfax Conduit', *Oxoniensia* 29, 1964, p. 142

North Leigh Roman Villa

Henig, M and Booth, P *Roman Oxfordshire*. Stroud: Sutton, 2000

Percival, J *The Roman Villa – A Historical Introduction*. London: Batsford, 1988

Wilson, D R *North Leigh Roman Villa, Oxfordshire*. London: English Heritage, 1988

FURTHER READING AND WEBSITES

Uffington Castle, White Horse and Dragon Hill, Wayland's Smithy

Miles, D et al *Uffington White Horse and its Landscape.* Oxford: Oxford Archaeology, 2004

FEATURES

The Prehistoric Downland

Drewett, P, Rudling, D and Gardiner, M *The South-East to AD 1000.* London: Longman, 1988

Drewett, P *The Archaeology of Bullock Down, Eastbourne, East Sussex: The Development of a Landscape,* Sussex Archaeological Society Monograph 1. Lewes, 1982

Leslie, K and Short, B (eds) *An Historical Atlas of Sussex.* Chichester: Phillimore, 1999

Volumes in Light – Buildings of the Modern Movement

Allan, J *Berthold Lubetkin.* London: Merrell, 2002

Powers, A *Serge Chermayeff: Designer, Architect, Teacher.* London: RIBA Publications, 2001

'The Modern House Revisited', *Twentieth Century Society Journal* 2, 1996

Yorke, F R S *The Modern House in England.* 1937

The Industrial Heritage of the South East

Haselfoot, A J *The Batsford Guide to the Industrial Archaeology of South-East England.* London: Batsford, 1978

Falconer, K *A Guide to England's Industrial Heritage.* London: Batsford, 1980

Crocker, G (ed) *A Guide to the Industrial Archaeology of Surrey.* Association for Industrial Archaeology, 1990

Eve, D *A Guide to the Industrial Archaeology of Kent.* Association for Industrial Archaeology, 1999

USEFUL WEBSITES

www.berkshire-archaeology.info
(Berkshire Archaeology Research Group)

www.buckscc.gov.uk/archaeology
(Buckinghamshire County Council)

www.britarch.ac.uk
(Council for British Archaeology)

www.the-cka.fsnet.co.uk
(Council for Kentish Archaeology)

www.english-heritage.org.uk
(English Heritage)

www.fieldclub.hants.org.uk
(Hampshire Field Club & Archaeological Society)

www.kentarchaeology.org.uk
(Kent Archaeology Society)

www.molas.org.uk
(Museum of London Archaeology Service)

www.nationaltrust.org.uk
(National Trust)

www.oahs.org.uk
(Oxfordshire Architectural and Historical Society)

www.sussexpast.co.uk
(Sussex Archaeological Society)

www.surreyarchaeology.org.uk
(Surrey Archaeological Society)

www.C20society.org.uk
(The Twentieth Century Society)

www.rdg.ac.uk/AcaDepts/la/silchester
(The University of Reading (for Silchester))